MW00571329

Dreams

An Thology of Wild Fiction at Wizard Academy

Edited by David S. Freeman, Peter Nevland and Scott Fraser

Austin, Texas

Printed in United States of America.

Wizard Academy Press
16221 Crystal Hills Drive
Austin, TX 78737
512.295.5700 voice, 512.295.5701 fax
www.WizardAcademyPress.com

Ordering Information

To order additional copies, contact your local bookstore,
visit www.WizardAcademyPress.com, or call 1.800.425.4769
Quantity discounts are available.

ISBN 978-1-932226-67-6 hard cover

Library of Congress Cataloging-in-Publication Data

2008938871

Dreams.
Dreams: an thology of wild fiction from wizard academy/ edited by
David S. Freeman, Peter Nevland and Scott Fraser.
p. cm.
ISBN 978-1-932226-67-6

First printing: November 2008

About the Cover Artist, Eric Fortune

www.ericfortune.com

The cover picture is a reproduction of a painting called "Dreams." Light and shadow, color and the void that colors fear — all of these exist in our world. You let them into your house, and they, in turn, open the ancient door to theirs. The restless wind in your heart is nothing more than the desire to trade places with light. But when you dream of color, where does that color exist? When you dream of light or the mischievous darkness, where do they exist? Dreams are nowhere, and everywhere. Perhaps you're in one right now, and Eric Fortune is painting you.

CONTENTS

In 2000, I challenged the students of Wizard Academy to:

1. log onto a secret website,
2. choose one of the candid snapshots they would find,
3. write whatever words the image inspired.

The result of that experiment was a coffee-table hardback called, **Accidental Magic**, *The Wizard's Techniques for Writing Words Worth 1,000 Pictures*. The book featured the work of 106 students and was sold in bookstores across America.

In 2006, I wrote, "Humans are peculiar creatures. We are capable of much, yet do little. Doubt, insecurity, fear and ambition blind our wide-open eyes to the colors of meaningful life. We hibernate, deep in the bellies of our comfort zones... Do you want to expand your world? Meet interesting people? Learn about different cultures? Then get on your hands and knees, drop to your belly and squirm under the fence that surrounds your insulated life."

I asked 32,000 readers to "arrive and be seated in a 24-hour eating establishment between 1:30AM and 5:30AM in a part of town where you rarely go. The more it scares you, the better." I said they should go alone and send me an email about their experience.

I expected 12 emails, but received 143. So we pasted them, exactly as written, into a marvelous book titled, **People Stories**: *Inside the Outside, Conversations Overheard in the Middle of the Night on the Wrong Side of Town.*

In 2008, I asked David Freeman, Peter Nevland and Scott Fraser to gather the sharpest knives in the drawer, hone them for 2 long days, then throw them up into air and cover their heads.

This book is the result of that adventure.

Hang on. It's a wild ride.

Roy H. Williams

Chancellor of Wizard Academy
and *New York Times and Wall Street Journal*
bestselling author of **Destinae**
and the **Wizard of Ads** trilogy.

Introduction

The sweet furnace of summer was melting streets and minds in the quirk-fest that is Austin. For absolutely no good reason that anyone could think of, a group of total writing novices gathered for an unorthodox (code word for "insane") two-day writing class called "Wild Fiction."

The workshop description promised, "This class is a wow-pow antigravitational joyride. By the time it's over, your creative talents will be tuned, you'll unsheathe the swords of beauty, danger, and irony, your mind will be on fire and some of you will see around corners... On the thrill ride of life's grand carnival you'll be the tattooed maniac whose hand is on the speed lever."

The class unfurled at the speed of a crazy bullet, as techniques were taught on bending language, on exploding the moment, on using words to stop time, on plumbing emotional strata, and on other chunks of wizardry that linguistic gunslingers need but which aren't taught in school.

What did this group of novices do with these one-way tickets to creative pandemonium?

You'll see...

David Freeman
freeman@dfreeman.com

Ruth Gilbert is a thirty-something someone who will never look a day over 29 even when she is no longer a thirty-something. She is the Mother of 2 beautiful daughters and a beautiful husband and bunch of fellow advertising executives that she learned everything she knows from.

Except for everything she knows about sex which she read about in either the Bible or Cosmo.

She's been to almost every state in the country and visited 6 of the 7 continents and 2 planets and given up several opportunities to go to the moon so that she could invest more time writing true stories that she markets as fiction.

Her favorite foods are organic red wine and chocolate chip cookies dipped in coffee with lots of cream and real sugar.

Someday she hopes to trade in her diamond ring for the biggest cubic zirconia she can afford. If there is any money left over she would like to buy a second house on the water to have a quiet place to write.

Someday she will probably be a vice presidential candidate for the soon to be formed Unaffiliated Voters Who Care About America Party - at which time, you will learn much more about her personal life than portrayed here.

Ms. Gilbert values people over animals, loves her Mom and her sisters and believes in God and hopes you do too. She also believes in 2nd chances (3rd and 4th too – but once you get to 9 or more – she's not really sure.)

The Back of My Hand

I hold few memories of my Pop-Pop. None fond.

I was one of those little girls they'd cast in an Oscar Mayer hot dog commercial. Cute as a jar of buttons.

My Dad's Dad was honoring us with one of his rare and unexpected visits. I don't think Marlboro or Jack Daniels would've ever cast him in one of their ads, but he lived on a steady diet of both.

Daddy does his ritualistic tinkering in the garage. Mom is just finished cleaning up the kitchen after dinner.

She fried fish that Pop-Pop had caught or swiped that afternoon. Everything else was from our garden. I helped Mom husk corn and shell lima beans at the picnic table outside while Pop-Pop cleaned the fish on yesterday's unread newspaper.

I watched quietly – paying mind to my own tasks as scales landed in his hair and on his stubble covered cheeks. He was tall, but shorter than my Dad which didn't seem right. His skin was red and there were purple capillaries that had exploded just beneath his skin that fascinated me. He wielded the oversized fillet knife un-masterfully and at each opportunity taunted me with the fish guts and he would have convinced me they were my dinner portions if it weren't for my Mom's continued validation of otherwise.

Dinner is done and the kitchen is cleaned. **A heavy smell of fried fish still lingers. The windows are open, but not a breeze dares to sneak in.**

Dad's already in his garage and the three of us go outside.

My Mom leaves me to sit with Pop-Pop on our back steps for a few minutes while she goes to the fence to give our neighbor some extra tomatoes from our garden. It's that time of year when they're multiplying. We eat them on sandwiches at lunch; sliced, stewed or fried for dinner. We freeze them and can them, sauce them and soup them and eat them like apples. We give them away – but NEVER do we throw them away. If one of them is starting to think about turning bad – it goes into the fermenting pot to be handcrafted into the finest South Jersey Tomato wine you could ever imagine - according to the few who dared to taste it.

I had really wanted to go with my Mom. I loved Betty Turner. She was the best neighbor a little girl could have. She was short like a kid and fat and pretty with short thick silver hair that used to be long and black. She had eyes like a doll baby and she wore lipstick every day. She had 3 grown sons and she always wanted a little girl just like me. She gave great hugs and smelled like vanilla ice cream and she usually had Hershey's kisses in her apron pockets that she'd let me reach in to find. Her laugh was so high pitched you'd think she was faking it, but that was really just how she laughed. She and my Mom were friends and still are. She could have been married to Santa.

I was sitting between his legs. The roughness of the brick steps imprinting coarse designs on the backs of my little pork chop thighs. I'm leaning back on him, cradled against his body, occasionally draping my arms over his thighs for support as I watch my Mother talking with Betty. I am sure she's complaining about something Pop-Pop said about her cooking or her legs. I'm impatient for her to come back – she'd promised strawberry short cake for dessert and I want to go see what she and Betty are talking about.

I start to squirm and thought about jaunting across the grass to see them when I hear her laugh. The steps are hard and Pop-Pop's not such a comfortable backrest anymore. He smells like wet dirt and medicine and old tin ashtrays. I try to stand up for the second time and he gently pulls me back with just enough firmness to get me back and settled. He takes my little hand into his big calloused mitt. He leans in putting his mouth to my ear and speaks quietly and authoritatively from behind me. "Hold still."

I wiggle and giggle because I think I'm about to *escape*.

He holds my hand way too tightly now. I grimace. This time louder "I said hold still little brat."

I go paralyzed as I watch him push the end of his cigarette into the back of my right hand.

The heat shoots as quickly to my cheeks as it does to my feet and I break his hold and run for my Mom, screaming.

I hold the assaulted hand in the other as if it's an unattached object and look down at it as I jolt across the yard. There's gray and black ash smeared over it with a shiny section of exposed flesh about the size of a pencil eraser and about the same color – just brighter. There's seared skin that shrunk up and pealed away surrounding it. I'm expecting some blood, but there's barely a trace – just a red string of thread that frames the tiny wound – separating it as a boundary between the pink exposed flesh and the peaches and cream skin that covers the rest of my hand.

I can't raise my head to look at my Mother's face, but she kneels down to my level and sees. She whisks me up in her arms, abandoning Betty and trots me towards the house. I catch a glimpse of Betty standing at the fence dumbfounded with a bag of tomatoes in her hands as I bounce against my Mother's body - holding on with my good hand. I go into a wave of heavy bawling as I utter out that Pop-Pop burned me.

She rushes past him angrily – reprimanding as we pass. "God damn it Earl, couldn't you just watch her for 2 minutes. Are you so inebriated that you can't manage your own cigarette?!"

She assumes it was an accident.

He stands and watches as we go through the screen door. In the most normal and kind voice I've ever heard him use when speaking to my Mother he says, "I'm sorry, she was trying to sit on my knee and I was trying to balance her 'cause I didn't want her to fall on the steps and get hurt. I didn't mean to. Is she all right? "

I see him over my Mother's shoulder as we trail away. He gives me a wink and a knowing smile – he knows he's off the hook – at least for doing it on purpose. He's hoping I'll play along.

Upstairs to the only bathroom in our house, she puts me up to the sink and I have to stretch my arm for my hand to reach the cold running water. The change of sensation helps me to stop sobbing for a moment. My Mom moves quickly to find her arsenal of Bactine and Bandages and some old burn salve in a tin can that looks like Vaseline.

She tends to my hand and between sobs that occasionally evolve into hyperventilation, I tell her what really happened. Even about his wink on the way in. She doesn't believe me and starts taking his side.

Looking back, I know that she likely did believe me, but she was trying to shelter me from the fact that my own Grandfather would do such a thing. She went to a great deal of effort to re imprint the facts of the event into my brain with a nicer version of the incident which was labeled an accident. "Pop-Pop loved his beautiful little Granddaughter and he would never do such a thing – no Grandfather on Earth would ever hurt his Grandchild. You're just being a silly little thing."

Maybe she couldn't acknowledge the truth. Maybe she'd have felt responsible for leaving me alone with him. Maybe she just didn't have it in her to take it up with him or with my Dad. I had strict instructions not to tell my Dad that I thought Pop-Pop did this on purpose because that would just make Daddy madder about it.

I was the one getting madder. Madder by the second. I screamed to the top of my lungs. I screamed so loud that my throat hurt the next day – "HE DID IT ON PURPOSE. ON PURPOSE! ON PURPOSE! HE DID IT ON PURPOSE!!!!!!"

I hoped he could hear me.

I argue and explain. I plead for her to listen but she stifles me.

It gets to a point where I almost believe she is right and that I am wrong and that it was some sort of accident. Maybe I am crazy.

But she wasn't there. She didn't see him do it. She didn't feel him hold my hand still while he did it. She didn't hear his voice. She didn't see his wink.

My throat is thick and hot. This may be the first time in my life that I am truly angry. This isn't frustration. This isn't me wanting my way. This is my first taste of injustice.

I am a child unheard and alone. I hate him for hurting me. I hate her for not believing me. In this moment I hate a lot of the pieces of my little life.

Eventually, she wore me out – or I wore myself out. I had stomped and screamed and threatened to tell Daddy, but none of it worked. She said I was wrong, that I misunderstood the entire situation and if I told Daddy, then Daddy would beat Pop-Pop up and it would all be my fault. Poor Pop-Pop would get all beat up because of me and my hardheadedness.

I decided not to tell, but not to protect Pop-Pop. I justified it in my own way.

My Dad might have killed anyone - including his own father - if they so much as let me stub my toe – then he'd have gone to jail and then I might never see my big strong Daddy again. So to protect my Daddy from a life of prison, I decided that I wouldn't tell him the real story. My Dad would be safe and I could keep him.

A while later, after some cuddling with Mommy on the couch with ice over the bandage, I am able to relax some – even though I know deep inside that I am trapped in this false reality that my Mom created. I can feel my heart beating on the back of my hand as I drift off to sleep in her arms.

We never discuss it again – not even in the days that follow when she changes my bandage do we ever mention it to one another. Her tolerance of this injustice was sickening, but it was what it was.

The scar is still there and each time I look at it – I see a reason to listen to children and to be their voice.

There are a million wonderful facets to my Mother that I am blessed to have known. There are qualities naturally passed on to me and some that I hope to master one day. She was a salt of the Earth woman, not a perfect Mother, but the perfect Mother for me and today she is an esteemed friend. Unfortunately, her inability to stand up for me or even to validate me privately, damaged my sense of security in the world for a long time. It took me too long to learn to stand up for myself again. Way too long.

My Pop-Pop died a few months later. I remember that I wasn't greatly affected.

I did not cry. I had just turned 5 and I did not cry.

I did wonder if he was sorry for burning me and if he was – I wondered if he would get into Heaven.

I hoped God would not let him in. I hoped that maybe, even right then at the moment while I was thinking all of this that he was in Hell and the Devil himself was giving him a wink and a smile.

Maybe the Devil wasn't so bad after all.

Perhaps the Devil could be my ally and torment anyone else who might ever harm me. If my Mom wouldn't protect me and if God wouldn't protect me – then the Devil could deliver some justice.

Perhaps He could make my Pop-Pop be sorry for hurting me.

But I guess just like you can't make someone love you – you can't make them be sorry either.

That's how I remember him.

I doubt that's how he would have wanted to be remembered by his youngest granddaughter.

I came to forgive my Pop-Pop and my Mother as well.

The scar that was the source of many fast lies and a few honest moments immediately cringed upon, started to fade.

I wonder what kind of a childhood he had.

I bet he liked catching lightening bugs and building forts and his Mom's strawberry shortcake.

But I'm sure he had a few cigarette burns of his own.

Tonya Crews. Wordsmith savant and surfer of prose. Fiction and of fact and Kobayashi Blue. Personifies still waters that run deep. All housed in wisdom and grace and wit.

Frolic

Tonya Crews

Sunlight penetrates the tranquil kitchen causing the window to buckle under pressure. I am captivated with requests of inquisition and so, gaze into the glow of Wonderland's mirror. The millions of droplets that tickled the tree branches an hour ago, now glistening, bring daylight twinkle to the yard. A red robin puffs up his chest to serenade Mother Earth before taking to the delicate wings of the soft breeze. Emeralds of varying degrees paint a mosaic that compliments the evening backdrop of pinks and violets. Uneventful as this day displays on calendar, being present and fully conscious of the harmonious perfection of Earth's relation to all its creatures is nothing short of pure majesty.

The dripping of life's richness instantly summons warm memories of my grandmother. Paralleling nature in its physical form, she was a mesmerizing light, a refreshing outpour of energy, a creature that sang and pranced to her own song, a masterpiece draped in vibrancy, a spirit in harmony with abundant glory. Her story is one of laughter and light-hearted joy, simple pleasures and extravagant escapades; succinctly: existence fully expressed.

Dancing to her own tune was more than a cliché for grandma, rather a mantra. Quite literally in fact, as on many occasions her faint humming would waft through the home like succulent scents emoting from a 5th generation bakery at daybreak. Coupled with her vivacious passion for movement, traditional to modern, ethnic to conservative, she lit the floor with her captivating flare. It was no wonder her closet, lined with go-out heels and bedazzling dresses, was a kind of imagination and inspiration room for my sister and I, within which we spent hours in the hopes that a flint of her star-spangled life would seep into us. This facet exemplified grandmother's zest and solidified life's full dance card.

Thediminutiveframethathoused"LittleGrandma"deceptively and advantageously shrouded a powerfully opinionated, cunningly persuasive fox that commanded respect to the point of compliance. My father disdainfully recounts stories of her coercive nature on what otherwise might have seemed playful family excursions. Coyly, she voiced her desires with full expectation of their manifestation. Resistance, however threatening, was simply and immediately dismissed as if it floated on a foreboding tide that slunk ashamedly back into the sea. No amount of knowledge, aggression, determination or willpower trumped grandmother's convictions. She was a woman who knew what she wanted and by traveling the path of least resistance, always achieved what other's remotely savored in the highlights of their most delectable dreams.

Grandma possessed the strength to brave the arduous roads that befell the Depression era, and emerged determined on living unabashedly joyful. The potential upsets in her life were of little importance and the mundane nothing more than leftovers pushed to the back of her refrigerator. She fancied the cherries on top of life's ice cream sundaes; hers being large enough to invite guests to devour. My Grandmother was the original Auntie Mame.

Much like a blanketing forest with roots that intertwine and form a unified root system, we as humankind are bound to each other through our varied paths of experiences grounded in this physical life. As each individual traverses their path, they exhibit a menagerie of events that directly connect their world with co-conspirators. In this way, I have lived a multitude of lifetimes through my Grandmother's adventures, absorbing decadence of the most luxurious rapture. The depth of her character reflects a world not unique unto herself, as we all share the capability to enjoy the spoils of life experienced in its totality. Oneness lies in the roots of our foundation. Those of us, who are conscious enough to transcend our self-constructed boundaries, have a limitless plenitude of stories to create. In doing so, we come in alignment with the true nature of our being. Evidence of this illuminates Grandmother's journey and provides a trail upon which my feet can embellish. Concern yourself solely in expressing your truth and yours is a life drenched in heart thumping, laughter induced bellyaching and smile stinging, bliss.

OZ. A SENTIENT WITH MINDS SCIENCE-IMMERSED AND ARTS-IMBUED, MELDING INTO CONSCIENCE FOUNDED UPON THE FIRST ON THE RIGHT AFTER HANGING A LEFT AT JUPITER.

They Move Among Us

Oz Jaxxon

Night removed his top hat and sat among the dew. Day's arms spread, his children's delight upon all, as light of the Northern Exposure.

It was a day to behold.

The wall solaced the little one whose ribs were as bars tattooed with paper and wind. He meandered as a tri-ped plus one – **plippity-thump...plippity-thump...plippity...**

A bi-ped encroached and stilled his gimp. Bars was unsure of this one's intent.

The Kid's ninth hole was buttonless. The first button, homeless. His limpid lemon shirt disappeared into the abyss of jeans well-aged and gathered around his waist. He waddled past Bars.

Bars skimpered for extra safety but suddenly froze. Statued, he peered at the Stranger.

His stride was confident, as a Tamarian upon cobbled stones. Shadowed wind escorted his coat, revealing the single garment beneath that concluded at each ankle. A broad belt encircled his waist. Twice.

He was a man of some mass. The line of his jaw unmistakable. His eyes set as by a sculptor. His face wisdomed as the sunset over Mykosian plains.

Bars saluted him. Bones of tail thumped that rhythm reserved for deity.

In a nano, the Stranger was at my side, leaning inward. His words thundered across neural paths. Rippled my eyes. Seared my memory.

Just as quickly he passed, his course resumed. Confirmation came with a sly glance over my left shoulder.

His words reverberated. Bombasted. Echoed. So much in so little so fast.

Bars remained at salute with head directed toward the Stranger. Turning fully in that direction, only the Kid was seen as he rounded the building's edge. Pausing, he looked back, almost as if searching for the Stranger. Then he was gone.

I stood there for a moment. Staring, but at nothing in particular, enjoying the fragrance that crossed my path.

Baffled, though I understood his words. Wizened, but unsure why.

Turning just in time, I caught a glimpse of Bars as he disappeared between the buildings, a completed quadruped.

-//-

"How was your day, son?"

"Weird, Dad. Kind of weird."

"How so, David?"

"There was this homeless bum following me. Then he said something to this guy right after I passed him. I thought it was about me."

"Oh..." a father's concern in his voice.

"But after I took a few quick steps like you taught me, I looked back but he wasn't there." His young voice quivered.

“What do you mean, ‘He wasn’t there?’ Did he cross the street or something?”

“No, Dad. He just wasn’t there! It was like he just disappeared or something. Vanished into thin air. And that man he spoke to? When I looked back he was looking at me. He looked kind of lost, like he was looking for that guy, too! But that dude was gone; he just wasn’t there. Not anywhere! And I certainly wasn’t going to go looking for him. It was like he disappeared into the wall or something.”

-//-

Nathan loved his grandfather’s stories. But this one gave him the heebie-jeebies. Full of mystery and wonder, he pressed him to tell more.

“Pa-pa…are you saying the man disappeared? Like off the face of the earth or something?!”

“Yes, Nathan. He disappeared. Of that I am as sure as I am that you are here with me at this moment. You see, Nathan, the Stranger was an angel.”

“Really! How do you know Pa-pa?!”

When angels leave your presence a fragrance like the lilies of Naluma surrounds you.

Sean Claes was born very little when he was very young. He has accomplished so many things in his 35 years on earth that he feels that listing them out would just be boasting. So, he thinks you should let Google.com boast for him. Go to Google and type his name and you'll get something great – reviews, humor, interviews with famous folks, photography, even a song written about him. He's also writing about himself in the third person right now. Some would call that an amazingly inflated ego. But the truth is, he's really just a big gooofball.

Claes believes everyone should listen to Los Lobos' *Just Another Band From East LA*, Ruthie Foster's *Runaway Soul*, and Darrell Scott's *Aloha From Nashville*, in their lifetime. Because, music is a bridge to something greater. What that something is...well... it's different for everyone.

He is also so awesome that he's got his own fan club and even his logo (seanclaes.com) won a national award. He didn't design the logo, Rolando Murillo at San Antonio, Texas' Murillo Design, Inc. did... but it IS his name.

In all seriousness, Claes is seldom serious. Something his wife Jodie and his two greatest accomplishments (collaborations) ever, daughters Marlee and Harper, can confirm.

The Invention of a Lifetime – The Drewson Suitcase Television

by Sean Claes

When historians dip their proverbial quills into the inkwell of invention, chances are the name Peter Drewson (April 20, 1928 – January 3, 2005) won't flow onto the parchment paper. In all honesty, not many have heard of this inventor, and even less know the wonder of his creation. The *Drewson Suitcase Television*, a functional television combined with a usable suitcase.

My grandfather knew Drewson from the time he spent in New York after highschool and before joining the service. Several times in my young life, I always took for granted that history had preserved his story, but when I attempted to find him online one day, I realized that there was precious little to find about this man.

So, as a writer, I felt his legacy should be preserved. I was planning on scripting an entire book based on his life, but I was only able to get one interview with him before he passed away. The following is that interview.

Q&A with Peter Drewson (December 15, 2004)

Is it true you used to be a door to door salesperson?
I was a Watkins Man in New York City from 1945 - 1972.

Watkins Man?
Yes, I worked for the J.R. Watkins Company. I sold a variety of natural apothecary and natural home care products. Ever hear of Watkins Red Liniment? The company was founded on that. Not to give me a case of fathead, but in 1949 I was their 3rd top sales person in the state.

But you were also an inventor?
I'd been tinkering around since I was a kid. My father dabbled in short-wave radios when he wasn't working at the factory or at the track.

How did you come up with the idea of a suitcase television?
It was quite simple, actually. It's the best of both worlds. You can always have the television with you, no matter where you go, you'll never miss your programs. You see, I realized long before

the world embraced it… perhaps my biggest fault… that the little picture tube you see before you was the big escape. Escape from reality. Escape from the normal daily grind. Escape from your life. My plan was to make that release from normalcy mobile. You truly can take it with you.

It was a wonderful concept. It was the thing that was going to make me a millionaire. Everything would have been wonderful. The world would have bowed to me.

How many did you sell?
What kind of question is that? Oh… you're grandpa never told you, did he? I only had the prototype. Just the one. I never sold a damn thing. Fucking Sentinel releases their Sentinel 400 and it's a damn box with a handle. THEY got mass marketed in the late 1940s. I improve on their design and come out with something that is amazing AND practical and what do I get? Zilch. Those bastards at Sentinel wouldn't even take my call.

Motorola came out with a portable 7" too. But you see, the thing is.. it wasn't practical. The Drewson Suitcase Television was a two-in-one. That is practical. I met up with Ron Popeil at the Great New York State Fair in 1957 and he suggested I use Velcro to place a padded cover over the suitcase television. Still no bites.

Do you still have the prototype?
I assume it doesn't exist anymore. In 1974 I was on a train from New York City to Scranton, PA, drinking in the bar. I was pitching my invention to some folks at Packard Bell when a fire broke out. I narrowly escaped with my life, nine others weren't so lucky. I lost the suitcase television on that car.

While trying to reconstruct the suitcase television for a subsequent meeting with Packard Bell, they went out of business.

Then the advent of the personal computer hit the masses and my idea was suddenly old news. When William Moggridge released the first laptop computer in 1979, it was the end for my invention.

I slipped deeper and deeper into a depression and started to have severe anxiety. I didn't want to leave the house. I stayed indoors for months at a time, just working away at my inventions. Nothing seemed to work. But I wasn't ready to let go. If it wasn't for my uncle Howard bringing me groceries, I don't know what I'd have done.

So, where have you been since then?
In 1980, I had a complete nervous breakdown and my only living relative, my uncle Howard, found me barricaded in my home and checked me into the King's Park State Hospital. I was put on Thorazine and it adjusted my moods. I was found to be competent to live on my own in 1996 when King's Park closed. I moved into a home with Uncle Howard and when he passed away in 1998, he left me enough money to live comfortably for the rest of my years. I am still a salesman, but now I sell from my home via computer. All I need is a little food and my books and I'm fine.

I know, it's ironic. The thing that caused me to lose my dream allows me to earn a living now.

Shortly after this 2004 interview, Peter Drewson was found dead in his New York apartment. Autopsy proved that his prolonged use of Thorazine resulted in Neuroleptic malignant syndrome, which proved fatal since it was left untreated.

Jeff Sexton, not his real name, worked as script writer in the adult film industry business to make ends meet during college. He also was a professional vegan body builder (apparently steroids are considered meat) winning the Mr. All Vegetable body builder title twice. He short career as a NASCAR driver ended after a fist fight with Jeff Gordon (needless to say Jeff started it). He hitchhiked across Omaha one Saturday when he was a junior in high school. He worked as an undercover student ombudsman at the Iowa school for the creatively challenged. His work led to legislative changes regarding the IC Imagination Challenged. After winning a thumb twiddling contest at the University of Nebraska he was hired on the spot as the traveling banjo tuner for the Bluegrass Polka Band … a tragic "whittling accident" ended his career in music field. Currently he works as script consultant for the adult film industry.

Substance and Artifact

Angela Farnsworth awakened to a tie-dye tinged halo circling cold white halogen lights. Her first thought was a lazy, *God that's pretty,* followed by, *oh shit - please let that haze be temporary.*

Most patients opt for local anesthesia, but 'no way, no how' was someone going to shoot a laser into Angela's eye while she was awake to see it.

"Relax, Ms. Farnsworth, the glare is temporary. You'll only see it when you look directly into the light, and it should go away in an hour or two. The operation was textbook perfect; no need to worry"

Did I say that out loud? "I guess I said that out loud, huh?"

"No worries, Angela, you'll be fine."

That was nearly three hours ago. So far Dr. Bronner has turned out to be a liar. *Frank is sure-as-shit no point of light and even* ***he*** *has that damn bluish haze around him. It's not getting better; it's getting worse!* Angela e-mailed Dr. Bronner from her blackberry and continued to look down at the table, resting her eyes

She wanted to escape seeing it, that faint, misty corona surrounding the lights -- and now people, too, dammit -- kind of like what she'd see as a kid after swimming in chlorinated water for too long. Meeting her friends for coffee this morning may not have been such a great idea. The normally pleasant and homey clatter of coffee cups and silverware clanged in her ears and jarred her thoughts. Even the coffee smelled bitter and the steam from her cup fogged her sunglasses, forcing her to look back up at Frank.

"C'mon, Angela, take the rest of the day off for God's sake -- or at least your heart's sake. We'll handle your presentation. They're your slides and everyone knows it's your proposal -- who cares who gives the song and dance, right?" Frank looked directly at Angela as he said this but gestured to the world in general, as if it stood ready to vouch for his sincerity.

Did his haze just change into smoke? Angela rubbed her eyes and Frank's smoke/haze went away. "And I suppose you'd be the ideal song and dance man, right Frank? No I've got two teens returning to see me, and I'm not sure they'd make it back out if I rescheduled. Somebody's gotta be there to tell them the truth."

Sarah put her hand on Angela's. "I admire your dedication, Angela; you're always there for those people."

It's amazing how much you can like the wife and hate the husband, thought Angela. Even without eye surgery, Sarah practically glowed, and indeed, an aquamarine shimmer bathed her face for the faintest second before vanishing when Angela looked directly at her. Just then, the taste of half-digested biscotti came to the back of Angelas throat at the thought of Sarah crying out Frank's name in passion.

"Ugh-hem, thanks, Sarah. *God, is this coffee totally burnt this morning, or what?*

"Hey, I'm Just offering to do you a favor, babe" said Frank, as if reading Angela's mind and actively trying to prove the comparison with his wife. "It ain't like I'm the one who needs to get off the director's shit list."

His haze ***did*** *smoke over into an oily looking charcoal. That* ***can't*** *that be from eye surgery? Glare, yes. But glare that turns colors?* "Well that part's for sure. No, I appreciate it, Frank, but the proposal is good enough to stand on it's own and I need to see this through. Plus, I've got those two high-schoolers."

"Suit yourself. I'll see you at the proposal." Frank leaned over and kissed Sarah goodbye as they all stood to leave the table.

Actually, an oily smoke rather suits you, you backstabbing bastard. "Yeah, see ya there. Sarah, call me about tonight, OK. As long as Dr. Bronner isn't a complete quack, I should be fine for the movie."

On her way out the door, Angela decided to splurge for the cab rather than the subway. Too many lights and people. Outside, the city was in full swing: horns, traffic, and a bible-thumping streetcryer competed for earspace. People jostle Angela as she moves across the grain of sidewalk traffic towards the nearest cab. The driver is ensconced in a gauzy dark veil, as if night had fallen inside the cab, a miniature rolling darkness. Angela laughed. *I guess window tinting will do that*. Looking again at the driver, he was the same as any other cabbie in the city, wearing an open colored work shirt and black leather jacket, though he had his jacket zipped quite a bit higher than most cabbies.

Angela waved to the cabbie, saw he was available, and was about to get in when she caught another glimpse of the dark fringe, this time through a now-opened window. It was almost an anti-haze, sucking the light rather than fringing it. The hair on her neck stood on edge. The burnt and bitter coffee aftertaste sucked moisture from her mouth, and against her conscious inner-voice judgment of *you're being an idiot*, Angela walked towards another approaching cab and hailed it.

What difference does it make? It's not like I'm betting my life savings or moving to Sedona because of imaginary glimmers or anything. I'm just getting the next cab in the line rather than the first probably did someone a favor. Still, Angela felt funny about 'listening' to visual artifacts from surgery. She dialed Dr. Bronner from the cab.

"I see. So the haze and halos you're experiencing are changing shape and color? You know, Angela, it's possible you're having some kind of reaction from the anesthesia. As you know, we don't normally use general anesthesia for this procedure, so even though I've never had a patient mention that Are you using any kind of medication or other substances that you may have forgot to tell us about? Maybe an SSRI or antidepressant or something?"

Fucking great, he thinks I'm on shrooms and it's reacting to the anesthesia. "No doctor, I'm not on any kind of drugs or medicines other than the heart medicine I told you about the Plavix - it should be there in my file. And the halos didn't change shape, ok, they just moved or shimmered when I moved my head."

"But they did change colors, no?"

"Yeah, they did change colors, and even opacity."

"OK. Well, I'm going to transfer you to the front desk so you can come in first thing tomorrow, ok? We'll check you out then. I still think this will go away in another couple of hours, but we have to do a follow-up on you anyway and we don't want to take any chances."

"I understand. Thanks, Doc. See you tomorrow." *Damn, damn, damn. Now he thinks I'm a crackpot. And now I know this shit isn't normal. Fuck.* Angela slipped the phone back in the breast pocket of her jacket and got out of the cab thoroughly in need of her non-existent SSRI prescription -- either that or a drink.

Her sister's apartment had its usual, perpetually lived-in look. It was always just short of slovenly, in an endearing way. Jessica met her at the door, baby in one hand, phone in the other, and toddler in tow behind her.

"Hey, look at you Holly Golightly. Guess the temporary, plastic glasses weren't going to cut it, huh?"

Laughing, "like I wanted to look like some 3-D dork all day. Here I'll take them off for you." Angela slipped off her dark, designer sunglasses and was almost blinded by the blue coming from Jessica's arms. *Holy crap.* "Maybe I better put these back on." But the glasses no longer kept back the color. Her niece's aura danced and cavorted in front of her, joining with and flowing out of her mom's. *Oh my god…*

"So are those new, or are you still wearing your prescription sunglasses?"

"No, no. These are new for the surgery; no prescription required. Finally, huh? Only been talking about it for two years now" The small talk helped Angela keep from staring and gave her mouth something to do other than gape. But if she'd had any remaining doubts about what she was seeing this morning, the light coming from her niece put an end to it -- this was no eye-surgery glare.

Just then Angela felt her chest buzz and clutched at it, slumping against the wall, struck by the thought of stroke. *Oh, God. Maybe the anesthesia did have a fatal interaction with the Plavix. And now it's dislodged pieces of calcium and plaque, rattling like glass shards in my heart.* Cold sweat beaded on her brow and a vice gripped her sternum. *God, don't let me die. Not after I just started making my hard choices in life…*

Angela's chest buzzes away. Clutching at her chest, she feels it, just as her vibrating phone starts actually ringing. *Oh thank God!* It's Sarah. Pulling the phone out of her chest pocket, Angela answers, "Hello, Angela Farnsworth." You'd have never thought she'd just faced death from the sound of her voice.

"Oh thank Goodness!" Metamorphized by panic, Sarah's sweet voice sounded insectile, keening at her from her blackberry's earpiece. "Angela, how come you never called me back? Didn't you get my voicemail? We've been frantic."

"What the hell is going on? I mean no, I didn't get your voicemail; I must have been on the phone with Dr. Bronner. What is it? Why are you so frantic?"

"Turn on your TV – channel 4"

"OK. Hold on a sec." Angela turns to Jessica, who is clearly concerned at this point, "do you mind turning to channel 4?"

Jessica springs across the room to the remote, switches the TV on, and then stares at the image, slack jawed. "Go play in the your rooms girls…Now!" The children, sensing the urgency in their mom's voice, do as they were told.

The burnt out frame of a building, looking like a torched tinker-toys set, confronted them from the TV screen. An overturned taxi lay like a matchbox car thrown by an angry child, it's wheels sticking out sideways, breaking up what was once the building's façade and protruding into the sidewalk. Police had already removed the bodies from the scene, but blood splatters made it clear there were more than a few victims. Angela actually knew the place, a recently opened Pakistani restaurant, not a block from the coffee shop she'd just left. She'd heard some of her friends raving about their food the other day.

And then her heart stopped for a second time as the picture of a leather-jacket-clad cabbie flashed onto the screen. He lacked the dark anti-aura from this morning, but Angela knew instantly – knew this was the guy. Apparently he'd had explosives strapped to his chest and a bunch more in his trunk. He drove him and his fare straight into the restaurant and off to a previously-promised paradise. They wouldn't say who the passengers were, but looking at what remained of the car, Angela couldn't see how anyone could identify the passengers short of dental records.

Sarah's cricket voice continued in Angela's ear: "Angela? Angela! Listen to me, how do you know that wasn't meant for you? We saw you hail a cab down after leaving the coffee shop. We even thought it was THAT cab. I know you believe in what you're doing, but is it worth your life? Is it even making you happy? There are just too many crazies out there honey…"

But Angela had stopped listening. She couldn't move her eyes from the TV. She didn't even notice her sister moving across the room to hit the power button until the screen went black and Jessica was standing next to it.

"Uh, I'm gonna have to call you back, OK, Sarah." Angela killed the call and put the phone back in her pants pocket, away from her heart.

“What the hell is going on, Angela? Are you trying to tell me this has something to do with you? And now you’re here at my house!”

“No, it doesn’t have anything to do with me. I was at the coffee shop across the street from that restaurant this morning, is all. My friends saw me hail a cab and were worried about me. Then they freaked out when I didn’t answer my phone on the way over here. I’m not endangering your kids; I’d never do that. You know that.” Angela understood the fear, but was peeved at her sister’s implications.

“My God, Angela, you could have been in that cab...” Tears welled up in Jessica’s face. “Imagine if I had been trying to call you. Why didn’t you answer the phone when your friends called?”

“I’ve had some weird glare and haze since the surgery and I was worried. I called Dr. Bronner’s office just to make sure. I must have missed their call.”

“You didn’t tell me you had complications”

“They’re not complications. Dr. Bronner says anything I’m seeing should go away soon -- assuming post-surgery glare is what I’m seeing at all. Look, everything’s fine. I’m fine, really. I just came by to see you since Jack’s out of town.”

“Oh, thanks. I’m ok. Better even: Jack’s coming back tonight, a day early. You should have dinner with us. Lucy would be thrilled to have Aunt Angela over. And I’d be happy to have you close too, after that.” Jessica indicated to the TV.

“Oh, Sis…I’d love to, but I’ve got to go back into work this afternoon and then, since I’ll be way over on that side of town anyway, Sarah and I were going to grab dinner and see a movie.”

“Well, you be careful, there, crusader. I didn’t really hear much of your call with Sarah, but she’s right, you know, your work puts you in danger. And it feels like it’s taking its toll on you emotionally, too”

“Yeah, yeah. Look, I’ll be damned before I let a bunch of pinhead whack jobs intimidate me from doing the right thing, OK? I’m a big girl; I’ll be fine." It was a familiar refrain, for Angela, though one she normally said to others. And it was one that continued to echo in her mind as she walked through the doors to work.

Only 5 minutes till her teens would be in to see her. It was sad really, though all too typical. High school sweethearts fooling around, none too careful or smart. And now there was everyone in the world looking to piss their ideology into the teens' mistake, afraid to tell them about their real options.

Angela walked up to the door of the counseling room to join her colleague, Jane. She could hear the teenagers talking from behind the door.

"It's really an awfully simple operation, angel. It's not really an operation at all; it's just to let the air in. I'll go with you and I'll stay with you all the time. They just let the air in and then it's all perfectly natural."

"Then what will we do afterwards?"

"We'll be fine afterwards. Just like we were before."

Angela couldn't believe Jane was letting them go on like this. She walked into the room with the two teens and was met with a blaze of blue coming up at her from table height. *Oh my God!*

Angela walked back out of the room, pale and sweating, her sternum clenched in a vice. *Oh my God.*

Jane walked out to see what was wrong. "Angela, my God, you just scared the hell out of those kids. What's going on? You look positively ghastly… Look, it's like you always say, someone's gotta tell these kids their options, right? I know it's not as glamorous as pitching new locations to the director, but are you going to tell them the truth or not?"

Angela, slowly and with considerable hesitation, picked her phone out of her pants pocket and looked at it, thinking of her sister, her niece, the cabbie, Sarah and frank, and then pushed herself off the wall with her head, lengthening to her full height. *Oh my God… No, that's a path to madness; I can't go there now; I can't change the past...*

Slipping the phone back into her chest pocket, Angela gulped. "You're right, someone's gotta tell them the truth …"

Arden Singletary has lived in Atlanta, Georgia, Tallahassee, Florida, San Francisco, California, and New Orleans Louisiana. While living in New Orleans, she survived Hurricane Katrina, and heroin addiction. Currently living in a small town in Georgia, Ms. Singletary hopes to follow the example of nine generations of ancestors, and remain there permanently. She has been a reader and a writer for most of her life.

Don't Call It Possession

When I was a child, Papa would take me to the marina. The outboard motors left an oil slick on the surface of the black-green canal water that looked like the most exquisite rainbow when hit by the sun. The canal was man-made, a conduit between the marina and the warm, placid waters of the gulf, as green and clear and perfect as amniotic fluid. The outboard motors poisoned the canals like dirty needles, and the canal took the sickness to the ocean like the penis of an aids-stricken junkie.

Today I am as greasy as an outboard motor. While I lie in the bathtub, a helping hand slowly shoves me beneath the warm, welcoming bath water, and I imagine the resulting oil-slick is as captivating as the kaleidoscope of color on the surface of that diseased canal. I can open my eyes now and look up at the surface because I no longer wear the contact lenses that made everyone oblivious to my blindness, but stole my ability to open my eyes underwater. Glasses will suffice now. They are more convenient, and my lover finds me as enticing with glasses as without.

Staring at the quicksilver surface from beneath it, but unable to see any swirling rainbow of color reflected on it, I am lulled to sleep by the warmth of the water, and the warmth in my blood. The next thing I am aware of is a hand gripping me beneath my left armpit and pulling me to the surface, just as I have taken that first, seductive breath of water. I feel my right arm thrown over the forearm of the hand that pulled me from my drowning reverie, the same hand that pushed me underwater. Leaning forward across that arm, the one that holds me lovingly above my breasts, I begin to cough inhaled bathwater violently. When I am finished, the right arm that had been holding me transfers me to the crook of the left arm, and, cradling me like a baby, cleans my face with his right hand.

I am wrapped safely in Henry's arms, and he is bathing my passive body more lovingly than I have ever washed it myself. I feel the water from the sea sponge being squeezed over me, rinsing away the soap. The water trickles across my nipples, but I don't care about that anymore.

I remember buying that sponge in Tarpon Springs, a little town in Florida inhabited mostly by Greek sponge divers. There were sponges for sale all over this strange little town, in every shop, along with statues of Greek Orthodox saints, and tee shirts emblazoned with pictures simulating sodomy and catchy slogans all employing the word "Greek." I was most impressed with the giant, concave sponges used as a sort of tub for bathing infants. I can only imagine what it must feel like to be six months old, and lying in a giant, warm, wet sponge.

I am still languid, passive, and my blood is still warm in its vessels. This is not from the bath. This is from the passionate fuck that preceded the bath, the fuck that made Henry so civilized, so loving, and so thoughtful afterwards that he bathed me tenderly, and will now let me sleep undisturbed until I wake up on my own. I am every bit as satisfied as Henry.

Henry and I are not lovers, but we share a lover, and she is exquisite. Her name is Heroin. She has countless others who love her as passionately as we do, and eventually, we all give her everything we have and forsake everyone but her. Eventually, no one else exists, and one finds that one would cheerfully die for her.

Henry died in her embrace some thirty years ago, just before I was born. I never met him while his body still lived. Some passions are so all-consuming that those who are the slaves of those passions will remain "earthbound" rather than moving on to a place they fear they can never taste again the thing that feeds their hunger. Longing and lust can imprison a soul here, if "imprison" is really the appropriate word, for Henry has no desire to move on, or "go to the light;" or any such nonsense. Henry wants to get high, forever, and Henry can't, in his ghostly form, get high at all. Heroin doesn't dull the pain in your soul unless you have a body to put it in, with a needle, or up your nose. Henry has no body, no veins, no brain chemistry to be altered, no ability to make love to the great love of his life. This is the reason Henry needs me. I am still in possession of my smacked-out body, and I've become Henry's tool.

To get high without him was so different, I can barely remember what it felt like. I remember my first time ever, though. I was twenty-four years old. I had done just about every drug, and had a particular friendship with pharmaceutical painkillers. I'd seen the movie "Drugstore Cowboy" about a million times, and it was my fondest fantasy to rob a drugstore and hole-up in a hotel room getting as high as I could. At a party with my sister where being twenty-four made me already ancient, a crowd of kids were clustered in a tiny back bedroom snorting heroin. I bought my first twenty dollar packet, snorted it, and my "Drugstore Cowboy" fantasies became Golden Triangle dreams.

Henry is here, and he's not a dream, but he's just returned from somewhere with purer heroin than I could ever buy or steal without his help. I never call it "possession," because it's still my body, even when he's in it. I do the work before I let him come inside me. I find a place on my ankle that isn't too close to abscessing. As I push the plunger in, I begin to feel the warmth. This is my time, my only time alone with her. I pull back just slightly, and watch the blood swirl inside the syringe. Henry becomes impatient, so I finish the shot and prepare for him to enter me. I am high, and nothing is bad. I feel him slipping in through the top of my head. Once he's inside, it's like sharing a sleeping bag with someone. We lie together, embracing in the dark.

Dee Brian's nickname is Dee Brain. As a semi retired hitman for the poultry industry in Arkansas makes it dangerous to reveal too many details about her life. Plus she will blow a hole in my head the size of a small cantaloupe if I mock her. Chicken hit men have notoriously thin skin. She also knits novelty socks for NBA basketball players as a hobby.

She doesn't eat chicken.

Meteorite Retrieval

by Dee Brian

Bob and Earl had driven down the mistreated logging road as far as they could. They stepped into the back of the van and quietly slipped into their cocooning silvery attire. As they left, both were hoping that this would be a routine mission. The last few had been anything but.

Puncturing the forest, they sought the small rock that had plunged to Earth the night before. The quietude of the piney woods was fractured by the quirky tones of the gamma ray counter, the jostle of leafstalks and a sniggering twitter from a Blue Jay. As they closed in on their quarry the radiometer erupted with a tizzy of staccato banging.

Earl was the first to notice the limb that had been amputated from the tree as if a cannonball had smashed through it. In its wake, swatches of bark had been ripped from trees and boughs mangled, leading down to an insignificant pit in a clearing squarely ahead.

Bob cast his silver enclosed digits into the puny abyss but to no avail. They delved into the cavity with their shovels, making it more liberal until the meteorite was naked. Earl wrenched the rock from it's borrow with his spade. Bob jabbed his hand down to get the rock as if it might scurry away like a varmint. He held it aloft like a trophy won at the fair. Earl opened the lead-lined plastic box so that Bob could place what was left of the shooting star securely in it.

Neither said a word on the way back. Both were relieved that it had been a mundane assignment. The meteorite safely in its case was placed on a shelf in the van. Bob and Earl removed the stifling protective suits.

Earl turned the van around and they bounded down the abandoned logging road toward asphalt roads and civilization.

✠ ✠ ✠ ✠

Brilliance isn't a matter of gray matter ... it was a matter of conscience. The human mind responds best when you ask it to do something that defies gravity, and understanding. Set an impossible goal and unleash forces beyond your imagination. Logic is merely a monkey wrench for the mind. The same for words. As an engineer, author and artist **Mark L. Fox** approaches writing with the same unorthodox blend of knowledge and unfettered imagination. After working as a rocket scientist for 15 years Mark discovered the limitations of conventional thinking. As Mark says "The space shuttle is a bus, it's the destination that matters". A keen student of human behavior led him to write about leveraging Albert Einstein's genius in approaching everyday problems .... to be continued

Clifford's Day by Mark L. Fox

I was glad I had finally met my mother.

Death being inevitable, this was the final thought flash-frozen in my mind. My entire life did not flash before my eyes as others have attested. No vintage home movie marathon for me. Only a single Polaroid filled my thoughts.

Only now, 278 days later, have I instituted enough courage to read my own words. I share with you my experience of that awful, wonderful, humbling day. I am not even sure why I have decided to share this experience. Perhaps it might......well, never mind. These are my exact words as I wrote them that day.

The ground vanished like the ass end of a roaring Ferrari. Wind howling downward over my head and shoulders towards my feet. I could see my house rapidly shrink into all of Clarksville. Then Clarksville dissolved into something unrecognizable before every detail was blurred away. Nothing left to see but my feet trembling above a distant green-brown quilt.

Just a moment earlier I was enjoying my morning walk. The same walk I take every day to sort things out, sing with the sparrows, watch park kids ascend the splotch, and of course pet Harley. Simple things to keep me sane.

This is my time to relax. But not today.

I had no idea what was happening to me.

An eternity passed before I remembered to breath.

But when I tried, I couldn't.

It was harder than the hike to the peak of Mt. Chickaree. I was being squeezed from both sides. I could see my feet below me, but could not move my head, arms or legs.

This Sumu-side squeeze was hard to explain. It was nothing like anything I had felt before. Not like the one from Jennifer on prom night or the one from my Aunt Carol at the Tijuana reunion. This squeeze was heavy, but not in a bad way really. Slightly painful, but at the same time… somehow comfortable. A female hug is the only experience I can relate this feeling to. As I write these words, I know this makes no sense. Being completely helpless, this was my only comforting thought.

In a camera flash the pressure disappeared. The wind furiously switched direction like a Mad Hatter's Tea Cup Ride. The wind was now screaming past the bottom of my feet. I bent my knees in a fetal position and hugged my legs to keep the wind out of my eyes. I wasn't sure I wanted to see what was next, but closing my eyes made it worse.

The blue-brown quilt below me was instantaneously replaced with an unfamiliar view. It was a landscape of pinkish type sand dunes with metallic chrome caps. Mixed about the dunes were long, sharp, black stick-like objects. These black things were in stark contrast to the pink dunes. Then the black sticks vanished and the chrome cap dunes became less obvious as I continued to fall. Or was I really falling? Just because the wind was howling from my feet to my eyes meant nothing. I could be going any direction.

The white flash was the next thing I remembered.

Was I dead?

Impulsively my body gulped a cloud of air bigger than the day Tommy Rimes tried to drown me. Four more short rapid breaths and I realized I was lying on my right side. I leaned over to put my hand on the ground and tried to stand up.

But I realized instantly my hand was not touching grass or dirt. It was something else. Something different than I had ever felt before. It was more like a trampoline's surface, but not as smooth or as tight. That is the best I can describe it.

The surface appeared to look the same in all directions. As far as I could see anyway. There was nothing that resembled dirt, grass, trees or flowers. Nothing similar to Clarksville.

The ground tilted violently and I began to slide across the pink sand dune surface. I tumbled over 4 or 5 dunes before I saw the edge. There was no denying it; it was a cliff ahead. I scratched and clawed at the surface to try and get a grip. The surface was slightly slippery which made it nearly impossible to grasp. I tried to brace myself knowing I was going to fly over the edge. I closed my eyes. I didn't want to know what was next.

Slam.

I hit something so hard I swear I must have bounced up 2 feet from the surface. My neck cracked on the 2nd impact like the snapping of a branch.

This surface was different now. Cold, rock like with blue and white swirls. I still had no idea what was happening to me. Was this a crazy dream? If not, then let's put an end to this quick. I can't tolerate any more flinging, flying, flipping and falling.

The light kicked on like flicking the switch at 2:00 am. It was a very bright light, with an aquamarine hue. But this blue sunlight was not hot, nor was it cold. Actually it was a comfortable temperature.

Peek-a-boo eyes, drenched with fear not sparkled with play. Peering upward though the slots, I could now see the light source. Eight huge disks of light separated into 2 curves of four. Arched like one banana next to a twin mirror image.

For what seemed like hours (but I am sure it was only a minute or so) nothing else seemed to happen. I was just elated all the violent movement had apparently ended.

Then it occurred to me I might still be alive. In all this horror I had not encountered anyone or anything face to face. Nothing standing in front of me that I could fight. Then just like that, my kitten confidence became a lion.

Struggling to stand, "My aim is true" tattoo on my left ankle gave me the mental support I needed. I stared at the two blue-light semicircles. Then it occurred to me they appeared to be about the same size as the moon appears in the nighttime sky. Only much brighter than the flashlight image of the moon.

Then I saw something move in the center of the light circle. It was not a person. It looked like black crisscrossed twigs, like that of a bluebird's nest, but it was so faint it might be my imagination.

Then I lost my confidence as quickly as I had found it. I ran as fast as I could away from the lights. Looking back I was thrilled to realize the light circle was not following me. I was getting away. I wanted to live.

BAM!

I ran straight into something and was now lying on my side again. Breathless. What the hell did I run into? I did not see anything in front of me. There was nothing there.

In the distance I saw the formation of lights flying rapidly towards me. Damn it!

There they were, flying in a tight Blue Angel formation. Three gasps of breath before they were directly centered over me again. How could they move that fast?

Death.

Now there was no running from it.

Screw it.

Let them have their way with me.

Scared isn't the right way to explain it. That is what I expected, but not what I felt. This reaction was a complete surprise to me. I can not explain the emotion I felt. It was much more like anger or disappointment than fear.

There were so many things left to do.

Death dealt its final hand at a most inopportune time, I said to myself trying to think witty thoughts.

Why had I put off so many things? Why had I not taking those chances?

Now it was too late.

Again it was anger I felt, not fear. Why didn't we just buy that restaurant on Benson Beach? We could have afforded to get that loan. Sure the job at Stinson's paid less than Muldoon's, but the perks would have been worth it. Wow…the perks. I guess I'll never know.

What if I had gone back that night at Melinda's party? She really wanted me to but I was too hard headed. I had my pride you know. How stupid it seems after all these years to have let my ego get in the way. Young boy stupidity is obvious when you're no longer one.

Hundreds of choices a day. How can we know which ones are right?

I should have never taken it out on Mike's dog. I love dogs, but I hated Mike. I hated myself for what I did. Oh I wish I could take it back.

I wish it were easy to tell my dad I love him. It's just ……wow!

The blue flash lights flicked off. The air was replaced with a brownish haze. I looked up and could see the moon like circles overhead. They were not illuminated anymore but they were still there. All my attention was back on these persistent circles. For a moment there I guess I forgot I was dying.

Then the moon circles in lock-step formation flew rapidly away from me. Not horizontal like before, but rocketing straight up, vertically away from me.

Was I a fool to try and run away again?

I jumped to my feet and ran like hunted Beveren. I could feel a wall of pressure coming towards me. I could not see anything but could certainly feel it.

Then I saw it.

It appeared to be a new wave of ground flying towards me about 6 inches above the existing one. I hurdled over the edge nearly loosing my right foot in the process. Thankfully its movement froze just before my feet landed.

An instant rush of wind hit me from the right side. The horizon was swaying back and forth like a slow moving seesaw. I dug my hands into the ground. This surface was different than before, It had large tube like ropes twisted around each other that ran as far as I could see. I could get both arms around these ropes to stabilize myself. The wind was strong but not forceful enough to pull me loose.

Just as I was starting to feel relatively safe the entire ground jolted downward with my head way below my feet. My feet flipped over my head and I slammed my knees into the ground. I could barely hold on.

Then a violent vibration shook me like a paint mixer. I bit clear through my tongue and could feel the numb warm river of blood in my mouth. In an instant the shaking intensified and threw me straight into the air.

Again I was falling.

BAM!

I could not move. Surely my back was broken.

I must have been passed out for some time. The blood from my tongue had spilled out of the side of my mouth. It felt like dirt stuck to the side of my face.

Dirt?!

I rubbed my eyes and begged for them to see. Everything was a blur. Then finally I started to get my vision back.

Oh my god! Is that Margaret's tree? It is the only tree I have ever seen with a clover shaped branch. It looked just like her tree back in Clarksville.

It can't be it.

The lion was back. I somehow found the strength to get to my feet and make it to the base of the tree. I hugged it, not just to hold me up, but to fake myself into thinking I was home.

Then I saw it. Wilson park was right in front of me. I snapped my head to the left and saw the old Emerson building. This place looks just like Clarksville. Was I home?

Was this just a horrible dream?

Wilson park was only a couple of miles from my house. I started to hobble towards it.

The clock on top of the Chyten building read 8:10. How could that be? I left my house at 8:10?

To this day I can't explain why at that point I no longer felt I was in danger. Certainly the ground could disappear again just as easily as it did before. Were the blue moon lights coming back? My gut said no. Having no rational reason to believe this, I did anyway.

Why did this happen to me? No one will believe me when I tell them. Should I just keep my mouth shut? Everyone accuses me of exaggerating anyway; they will never believe what happened.

I could have died today but I didn't. I should have died but I didn't. Why didn't this thing kill me?

It is a small front porch, but it is ours. So are the wicker chairs. The cool afternoon breeze always combs you with coolness at the end of the day. Grandma was angry when I put in the rail for her. She needed it but didn't want to admit it. I guess we all feel that way sometimes. I love the flowers as much as the Yellow Jackets do. Most folks are afraid of them, but they don't bother me.

I wish Ashlee was still with us.

"What happened?
Why is there blood on your face?"

So I guess you could say that im pretty outside the "norm" for the average sixteen year old German-Cherokee girl from Kentucky. But i like to look at myself along with others as individuals instead of a group. The best way to explain my self is this, I am Shayna Dean Bluemlein. I enjoy life, i interpret life and i live my life, not someone elses. These stories are profound, and the people even more surreal. The best part about this is the uncanny thought that a teenager could ever utter these words, let alone create them.

- shayna bluemlein

The Power

by Shayna Bluemlein

The flaming skies of the outlands above him, shone brighter than ever. Before, he saw the skies as nothing more thanpuffs, like that of popcorn, but now there was more. An array of emotions flowered through him like the Nile. He believed, he truly believed in the power.

He had never opened his eyes to the beauty, the shame, the undying want for power. “Is there something more... something I must find?” he thought. Looking to the flaming skies one last time, he found the Truth. It overwhelmed him like a tidal wave.

He was gone, not dead. Ah, no, he was fully alive, with his father and brother standing by his side.

AMANDA WACHTEL IS CURRENTLY A JUNIOR DOUBLE MAJORING IN MATH AND ENGLISH WITH A MINOR IN ITALIAN AT THE UNIVERSITY OF ALABAMA. AS A NEW MEXICO NATIVE, SHE ENJOYS THE GREENERY OF THE SOUTH AND USING A "BUGGY" AT THE GROCERY STORE. AN ASPIRING WRITER, MATHEMATICIAN, PIANIST, DANCER, ARTIST, WORLD TRAVELER, INVENTOR, COMPOSER, AND HUMANITARIAN, AMANDA FINDS PLENTY TO KEEP HERSELF BUSY. WHEN SHE HAS A FEW SPARE MINUTES, YOU CAN FIND HER EATING A PEANUT BUTTER SANDWICH OR TALKING TO HER ROOMMATES AT THREE IN THE MORNING.

Saving Lesi

by Amanda Wachtel

"He's gone."
"No. No. It's not true."
The tears were falling faster and faster, colliding in wet clumpy sorrow as I fell to the ground, clutching the wooden shelves of the bookcase. Grief ripped through me as my fingers clawed at the titles.
I looked at the books with disdain, struck with tragic realization.
"This is so pointless! All of it. These books are trash!"
Everything I loved only minutes ago seemed coated in a sheen of uselessness. Objects can't convey feelings. They can't feel pain. I've never read anything as terrible as dying. It just doesn't matter. I did my best and it doesn't matter. He still died.
I jerked my head to the side, tearing away at myself as if I could banish my grief with strong enough movement. I was already on the floor but it didn't feel low enough. I wanted to melt. Sink into nothingness. Lie shattered on the ground.
How long does it take to get up? When is it okay to grab a Kleenex? That's the part they never show in the movies. I don't know. I never did.
Someone put me to bed after I exhausted myself with emotion. Probably one of the beefy boys down the hall that Laria always talks to. Not really a comforting thought, but I didn't really care.
I don't know how many days it'd been when my body decided to drag itself back to class. I used to love school, the infinite breadth of promised knowledge, but I can't make it meaningful anymore. I can't understand why it's imperative to read a stupid chapter when everything has fallen apart.
My eyes glaze over as words hang in space on my computer screen. Stacks of neglected homework eye me from the table. I fail to notice the wooden chair digging uncomfortably into my shoulder blades.
"Lesi. You should totally go! This is exactly what you need right now!"
What I need right now is Advil I thought as Laria shoved papers at my face. Studying abroad in Italy is nowhere close to a 24 hour pain reliever.
"Thanks Laria. I'll look at them right now."
I didn't. I shoved them in my drawer and went back to sleep. Sleep—the magician who creates a different life every night and saves me from

reality. Such a sweet escape.

"Have you seen any Keats around here lately?" a British accent behind me asked.

The thrift store had a surprisingly large collection of classics. I was on a more destructive bent—looking for a novel to tear up for my latest art project, a sacrilege even I didn't quite feel comfortable with.

The man looked about 30 with a charming face and exquisite eyes.

"No, I haven't seen Keats, but they have multiple copies of Poe."

"Ah, I see. You're a gloomy one. No happy person ever suggests Poe. I'm afraid gloominess is out of style this season."

Though his tone was lighthearted, his eyes bequeathed a knowing understanding.

Later, as I pulled at the corners of my napkin, I thought about how Poe was exactly my season at the moment. My eyes examined Clarson from across the table at the French restaurant he had suggested. I couldn't figure out why I had agreed to dinner. Deductive reasoning skills hadn't been making regular appearances lately. All I knew was that he wasn't old enough to be my dad, and that seemed to be good enough for me at the moment.

It wasn't love but it was a nice distraction. Something I desperately needed before I drowned at sea. I was apathetic at best, but he didn't mind, so thankful anyone would date a man with a 6 year old child. Shelly was a surprise but it was easy enough to pretend she was my younger sister and we got along well enough.

It's strange when relationships involve generation gaps. I didn't belong in his, but neither did I belong in his daughter's. I was stuck in no man's land, floating in a great abyss of uncertainty with only two British life rings to save me.

"Lesi, are you going to be my new mommy?"

I looked down at Shelly's expectant face and felt the beginnings of guilt stirring. She had quickly adjusted to my presence and I made a point to pack her lunch every day.

"No Shelly. Sometimes people are only meant to be friends for a short while. That's what your daddy and I are. We're one-month friends. "

Her small mouth quivered and I rushed to find words of comfort.

"But even though I won't be here anymore, I will always love you because you are a special and wonderful girl and you always will be."

"I'm going to miss you!" she cried and slung her tiny body at me in a giant hug. There we sat, cradled together in the timeless tragedy of looming separation.

A week later I blinked at my reflection in the cracked bathroom mirror. The pink was a hideous shade. The ugliness made me feel better for a moment. I had taken action and finally done something. Not exactly productive, but after all these months of doing nothing, it felt exhilarating. I swished my pink streaked hair back and forth, trying not to breathe in the toxic fumes. I know that everyone thinks I'm out of control at this point, but I'm not. The funny thing about out of control people is that we actually think quite a lot. I must be a conscientious rebel. Then again, maybe I'm not out of control. Maybe this is just planned destruction.

"You're failing Italian Lesi. I know you've been having a hard time lately but I just don't understand—you're practically fluent in the language and you're by far one of the best students here."

I fought to hide the tears that were pouring down my face as my Italian professor stared at me from across the table. I hate crying in front of people but that seems to be my newfound talent this semester.

"I've given a lot of thought to this and I think there's a solution that will benefit everyone. If you agree to take part in the school's exchange program and go to Italy for a year, I'll erase this grade from your transcript. It might do you some good to get a little change of scenery and the program desperately needs more students. If I were you, I would think very carefully about this. It's really your only option and I know how hard you've worked to have good grades. Whatever it is that has you so upset, don't let it ruin you. Get out and learn how to live again."

I nodded, hiccupping out my thanks between sniffles. I hadn't planned to study abroad, but at this point I didn't really care.

Standing in the airport I wondered how many other people were lost. Not in the sense that they couldn't find the terminal but in the sense that even though they had a destination, they still felt hopeless. There should be a special travel package—how to get your life back. I could use one of those.

I walked into the University and marveled at the arched corridors and sweeping staircases. Even my gloomy self couldn't fail to be moved by the historic architecture.

"Welcome to World Religions. Your first project will be to interview the local head official of your assigned religion. I'm expecting great things people."

My stomach knotted involuntarily as I shifted in my seat. I had been assigned Catholicism, a religion that never failed to give me the creeps. It made me nervous for some inexplicable reason. My dreams that night were dark and haunted by chanting and cloaked figures in stone passageways.

Sitting in the priest's office, I remembered what exactly it was that bothered me so much about this religion. A giant crucifix hung on the wall, bleeding eyes boring into me, daring me to sin. How can people

put these things in their bedrooms?
"You're not Catholic are you?"
The priest's words startled me out of my terrible daydreams.
"No, I'm not."
"Sometimes it's hard for people on the outside to understand our religion. They think it's all stuffy old traditions, enforced by dying old prudes like me."
I wasn't quite sure how to respond. I'm pretty sure anything would sound insincere considering he was right.
"You don't have to say anything. Just listen. Our religion may seem rigid to you, but you must remember there is great comfort in the known. Catholicism gives a framework to God that you can see, and that certainty has saved many.
You look inside yourself for strength, but if you're searching for something, that means you don't have it, and that's okay. Most people need someone or something else. People disappoint Lesi, but God never does."
That's right I thought—God doesn't just drop dead when you need him most. Walking out of the church I felt a small corner of comfort edging out my uneasiness.
I finished spell-checking my report and closed my laptop with a satisfying click. I hadn't gone out in months, but somehow the thought of staying in my lonely room that night seemed unbearable. I found my purse and headed off to find the nearest bar.
As I ordered my drink I let my eyes drift over the room, taking careful inventory of the regulars. The crowd was small and the place lacked the chaos I longed for. A sweater-clad man sitting in the corner caught my eye. He was reading a novel and his conservative American clothing screamed tourist. I shook my head, amused.
I felt conspicuous sitting alone with my drink, a living ad of what not to do in a foreign country. Sure enough, a sleazy looking guy was fast approaching from the darkened recesses of the bar, black hair slicked back against his oily scalp.
"Ciao Bella! You like to come home with me tonight? I have beautiful house. I make you wonderful dinner."
My body instinctively shrank away from the man and out of the corner of my eye I saw the tourist stand up quickly and shove the book in his back pocket. He walked up to us with purpose and slid his arm around me.
"Sweetheart. I didn't see you come in. Are you ready to go?"
His speech surprised me. Though his English was perfect, his Italian accent was strong and I realized my earlier assumption that he was a tourist was incorrect.

He turned to the other man.

"Excuse us. We're late to a concert. Buona sera."

I wasn't keen on leaving with a stranger but I couldn't exactly stay in the bar. I'd never been abroad before and the horror stories the study abroad office had told me of night ventures gone wrong kept replaying in my mind. Nevertheless, I followed him and stepped outside, my lungs gratefully inhaling the unsullied air.

"I'm so sorry to barge in like that, but that man is notorious for mistreating foreigners. I didn't want anything bad to happen to you. You are very beautiful and he is very rude. My name is Angelo."

Our hands joined in customary introduction and I thanked him for intervening. Though I was grateful, I didn't quite know what to do now and the situation was growing awkward.

"I know you don't know me, but you can trust me. I am a respectable man. I will get you a taxi to take you home now if you want. I don't want you to feel uncomfortable. You just looked like you needed saving."

That last word fell heavily on me and for a second I didn't answer. Saving—that was indeed exactly what I needed, though saving from myself, not a stranger. I looked up at Angelo and was stunned by a beauty I hadn't noticed before.

"Yes. Thank you. Thank you for saving me."

The cab was forgotten as we wandered down cobblestone streets together, laughing as minutes floated by unnoticed. Angelo had given me a priceless gift—my first enjoyable evening, the first time I was finally able to stop thinking about what had happened.

The next morning I washed the faded pink streaks out of my hair for good. I suddenly didn't like them anymore and they felt alien to me. Glancing to the left at my clock, I realized I was running late and hurried to finish getting ready.

I walked hurriedly the few blocks to school, hoping to make it there on time, though Italians are pretty lenient on the whole time thing. They're pretty relaxed in general, which is a pleasant change of pace. I swung open the brick of a wooden door and gasped to see Angelo waiting inside. Our meeting wasn't planned and yet it felt like the obvious conclusion to last night.

As the weeks lazed onward, I spent my afternoons lounging on stone benches, studying with Angelo under the watchful gaze of marble statues and beady-eyed pigeons. I helped him uncover the mysteries of math and he taught me the finer points of Italian—and Italians.

Stepping into the piazza, I could see Angelo waiting for me. Our morning espresso was quickly becoming the favorite part of my day. I felt bad for the old woman sitting alone at the corner table. I had no

desire for solitariness, no longing for that "alone time" that is so exalted these days.
"Lesi, we're running out of time. The school year is almost over."
It hadn't struck me how little time I had left, just over two weeks. Maybe I had realized it deep down, but I had carefully buried the acknowledgement so I wouldn't have to face the truth. The truth was I was in love, and I couldn't bear the thought of going home.
"You don't have to leave. Please stay here. Stay with me."
I thought about how easy it would be, how perfectly simple to never go home, to live in a dreamworld of happiness where reality is forgotten. Yet instantly I knew I couldn't.
"Angelo, I can't. I have to go back and fix the life I left behind. I need to graduate, to see my family, to make amends. I left everything in a mess and I can't stand to disappoint people anymore.'
"They'll understand. Life happens. We happened Lesi. You are more important than anything else. If you can't stay, then let me go back with you."
His pleading was painful. There was nothing more I wanted than to stay together, but I couldn't ask him to move to the U.S.—he was very close to his friends and family. I couldn't bear to tear him away from everything. Resentment seems to have a way of seeping in over the course of time and I didn't want it strangling us in the end.
"I will come back. I promise."
His head fell forward and his eyes clenched shut against my words. We knew this is how it would be, but it never hurts to try to alter the unconquerable course of fate. It shows a dramatic type of purpose, a striving that makes us human.
We spent my last night in the countryside, laying on our backs and looking into the timeless stretch of stars, swatting at mosquitoes through the thick air.
"Lesi, promise me you'll come back soon. I can't live without you."
"I promise. You're my soul mate. We have to be together."
"What is a soul mate? I don't know that word."
I thought about it for a while, trying to choose the right words to make him understand the importance.
"A person's soul mate is the one person in the world that was made just for them. The person they were born to be with. The only person who can complete them."
I felt him smile through the darkness and a new calmness settled in.
"Yes. We are most definitely soul mates. "
The taxi ride back to the city seemed accelerated, precious seconds zipping by at hyper speed. The airport loomed in the distance and reality

drizzled sadness upon me. This was the last moment I would spend with Angelo before uncertainty took over.

Rolling my luggage into the airport, I fought back tears.

"You have to stay here Angelo. If you come any farther I won't be able to leave. This is too hard as it is."

He wrapped me in a final hug, his arms expressing the urgency of my return. I pulled away and ran up to the ticket counter as the monsoon of tears began to rain down. It wasn't fair that I was choosing to leave the one person who mattered most to me.

On the plane I slumped down deep in thought. Mentally calculating plane ticket prices from the U.S. to Italy, I wondered how many part-time jobs I'd have to get to pay for them. Missing Angelo was instant and I knew I wouldn't be able to stay away for long.

Back at school I collapsed on the living room couch, luggage sprawled across the room. Laria came and sat down beside me. It was different now, the mood had shifted. When I left my heart was shattered by the hand of death, but since then I had rediscovered life. It was still hard though. Angelo had put me back in order, but sometimes loving is just as hard as losing.

I let a sigh escape into the stillness of the room and Laria wrapped me in a hug, fully understanding the meaning of my small utterance. We were both remembering that awful night over a year ago.

"Oh sweetie. I know it's hard but just remember—you've learned something that everyone else our age might not learn until a long time from now."

"What's that? What did I learn?" I asked. I had no idea what she was talking about.

"You learned that people aren't taken away from you because the world is out to get you. People are taken away to make room in our hearts for the really important ones."

I leaned my head against Laria's shoulder. Though the future sat in mystery, she was right. Angelo had more than filled the empty space in my heart.

Before I begin, I would like to thank the inventor of Spell-check, for without it this would be indecifurrable. I type slowly as my digits do not conform to the keyboard. It is a dogged task.

My best friend Rick Copper has spent Gumpian time with people from William Wegman to Farrah Fawcett, Muhammad Ali to Wayne Thiebaud, Bill Clinton to Walter Payton.

But he slurpees time, sucking it up writing 30 and 60-second blocks, suffering from brain freeze. He should use his fattened witty tongue, cork this flow, and re-direct it writing fiction or spend more time with me, his Defecation Sensation (don't ask me what it means, too many syllables).

He wants to have to work figuring out the exact day of the week. He wants to write as thoughts come. He wants to listen to Warren Zevon whenever he desires. He is splendid with isolation.

Such is not the case.

Every weekday, he commutes.

Every weekday, he faces the nameless throng slowly stampeding into the office.

Every weekday, he drops his sack lunch in the office fridge, thinking about my sad-sac hazel eyes.

He tells me all he wants is for me to be happy.

I need to go now. I see fireworks in the distance.

I must protect the house from their noisy blaze… and make poopsicles.

Honey Copper
Foxfire Red Labrador, Rick Copper loyalist

PLUCK

One fall day before she slip-n-slid down nature's canal, her mother's brother, Artie, turned spontaneous rehabber. He started at his house's corner, sledge hammering exterior bathroom walls papered in faux olive green ivy with thin salmon veins. Today, the rickety house, façade of a stroke victim, begs for a load-bearing post and a paint job.

During a short summer, Uncle Mortimer, her father's side, started a grease fire in the kitchen skilleting turkey eggs in a week's worth of bacon grease. At three-toed sloth speed, he half-jogged, grabbed the garter snake-ribboned hose, spritzed through the window screen, flaming the fire further toward furniture. He could have saved the kitchen, dining room and living room if he had called 9-1-1. Uncle Mortimer claimed his phone was factory-flawed.

Damn Ma Bell forgot to put an "11" on the rotary.

In spite of this inauspicious genealogy, Andrea was considered a bright girl. Bright enough, despite constant failure to garnish persuasion, public school was not deemed for her. Bright enough she knew as mother spent most of Andrea's waking hours telling her she wasn't bright enough, she was.

Andrea loved the thought of the school bell's chamber echoing the beginning of another knowledge-crammed day. She devised a deviously simple plan to attend school without anyone's knowledge. She'd get a bicycle. Regardless of the three miles of unkempt dirt roads, it needn't be a mountain bike with big man's whiskers nubs on knobby tires. Any old bike would suffice.

Her mother, so slender the whisk in her hand looked obese, was the defining matriarch. She made herself after Lady Bird, a woman currently whipping up her swan song from DC as her husband's heart was breaking from a failing war. Standing over an avocado ceramic pot over-steaming with red-skinned potatoes made mother closer to the physical apparition mother's mental state always held.

Slight build, but – according to Andrea – with hindquarters to match an African Water Buffalo's (partially to her lack of physical activity, mostly to her father's porcine physique), Andrea wasn't quite the saggy-fleshed stick as hyperthyroid mother. Ergo, Andrea surmised, not only would a bicycle get her to school, it would snag her much-needed exercise.

Mother was far from enthused.

"Have you seen your friend Emilio's bicycle? Good God, it's a death machine. Those pedals look like eel teeth, two wheels are unstable as it is and did you see that kickstand? It's like a prisoner's shiv."

The spoon, potato starch filmed balsam, waved a centimeter in front of Andrea's nose. Her violets volleyed as the spoon hypnotically tick-tocked.

"I know shivs."

4 days a week since Andrea was a fetus; mother would suit up, khaki green button down, black boot button up, to patrol the prison exercise yard.

"Do you realize the damage a kickstand can do to a foot? Imagine, that little sharp edge slicing open your foot like grandma's "as seen on TV" knife did her finger. Remember?"

As vivid as a Lemon Meringue Pie against a late afternoon South Carolina blue sky. The blade sliced through the first knuckle faster than Grandma Mae could shout 'shee-YIT.' Before she got to YIT, a third of her pointer finger was toggling amidst a cord of cut carrots.

Mother was more cautious, slicing slower, deliberate. All carrots were cut equal, prepared every Sunday as if the Galloping Gourmet would trot over any time for inspection.

"I have shoes, mother."

"Canvas. A Rhino could stick his horn right through those flimsy sneakers and..."

"That you bought for me."

"Don't get smart with me. No bike."

No bike. No skateboard. No scooter. Nothing to lock up side-by-side with other kids' bicycles on a static shotgun metal gray sine wave located 100 pre-teen's steps from the Andrew Jackson Middle School playground.

"If I can't have a bike, I want to go to school. Any…

She resolutely interrupted. Andrea had learned not to wait for retort to mother's diatribe on the detriments of public school.

any school, mother."

After machine-gunning public school negatives, mother, a daily vacant precise 12:10 train, rolled on with an unwaveringly weak solitary example.

"Your brother went to school. What good did it do him?"

Andrew Charles, aka Drewdle the Noodle, dropped out after 5th grade. From a family where Cap-n-gown in the closet was as far more rare than a full box of Cap'n Crunch in the cupboard, 5th grade was nearly an accomplishment. Truth was Drewdle's lack of functional brain matter had less to do with school, more with an attempt shingle-surfing his plastic oxidized blue sled off the roof into their backyard pond beyond the raspberries. He missed by only 25 feet, sloshing his brain into his eyeballs as he belly-flopped onto Kentucky blue before sliding to a stop staining his skin raspberry red. Lucky for him, if having an I.Q. a rung higher than a raspberry the rest of your life was lucky, there's was a ranch house.

"Andrea, I'm making Sunday dinner here!? Go outside."

"Mother…"

Andrea sighed and walked. Nothing interfered with mother in mid-Sunday dinner prep. Mother wouldn't miss anything for a long while anyway, mostly Andrea. Andrea heard mother's familiar sing-yell bounce off the hall walls as she snuck into her laboratory/ bedroom, clutching her prize.

"I am in the middle of Sunday Dinner, dammit Andrea! Play on the highway."

If it didn't say on her birth certificate Andrea Charlene Bickerman, no one would know her first name wasn't Dammit.

Sundays Grandma Mae made her weekly appearance adorned in flowing Aster dress. The two perpetual bachelors, Uncles Artie and Mortimer, parked their oft-shirtless denim-overalled carcasses at the kitchen table. Finally, in squeezed the four immediate family members. Often they'd wedge in one of the other prison guards who'd regale Andrea and Drewdle with tales of the sweet science of handling the incarcerated.

"Knuckles out, thumb in."

Andrea entered their grey matter slick as a fox into a henhouse, asking questions she knew the answer and ones she knew they didn't. Drewdle drooled on a crescent roll.

"Why thumb in?"

"If you don't you may jamb it on a cheekbone or skull."

"So you might break it?"

"Anyways, you take a stance. Low. Bend at the waist. Don't give them nothing to hit. Come forward eyes up."

"Do you think the South Carolina Penal System rehabilitates well compared to other southern states?"

"Always got the questions."

Andrea answered her questions reading. Mostly science. Not the science of pugilism. Science. At the age of 11 she had exhausted mother's scientific intellectual capabilities and the uber-genius of all Bickermans, her father. He made it through eighth grade. While supportive in his own 'stay-out-of-the-path-of-your-mother' method, father wasn't one to buck any matriarchal system.

"Why not?"

"School's no good. That's why."

"I can't learn anymore."

"Oh, you've just started."

"Can you teach me about the Theory of Relativity?"

"Always be nice to your relatives."

Her father laughed. He always laughed whenever he had no clue what Andrea was talking about. He laughed a lot.

"Besides, as I have said before, you're too pretty for public school. I shudder to think. Just shudder."

Father's greatest gift, flattery, denied the mirror's invention. Twisty auburn licorice strands covered a head carrying a nose only a prizefighter could envy. Twin violet eyes buried behind a smallish set of brown-framed specs beer bottle base thick. Masking tape made the pair one.

Pretty defined her room. Wall-to-wall stacks of books. She collected book-spending cash weeding out Mr. Twiling's rose gardens, taking out Mr. McGilly's trash Mondays, and walking the Gerranger's Boxer-Whippet mongrels.

Science dominated, art came second. She was Van Gogh with 2 whole ears, Einstein without the philandering. Reading for pleasure was foolish, although she had picked up *Old Man and The Sea.* She felt it would help her pick out proper tensile strength fishing line.

She plopped her procured prize onto her oversized pillow. Father's slightly rusted toenail clippers – clipped by Andrea a week ago to clip wires for her homemade radio that could reach Charleston AM stations if you set it on the sill pointing southeast – kissed the tips before its jaws snapped, exposing translucent cartilage.

The pages holding Newton's Third Law were close to disintegration. First draft a fantasy, Andrea burned through two pink pearls refining fantasy into reality. Success meant precise calculations. Failing to do so could result in what Andrea dubbed the Sunday Dinner Casserole Calamity.

"The force was right, mother."

"Nothing was right, Andrea. You owe me."

"You don't get it."

"No one gets it, toots. Green Bean Casserole is gone! China… China is broken!"

"And monks dance in Tibet!"

"Andrea Charlene, I don't get… sometimes if you…"

"You snuck in and set the green beans down! The china would have stayed put."

"If you weren't… no allowance!"

"Allowance? I get an allowance?"

Andrea remembered seeing mother's eyeballs push into her eyebrows as the marbles pinballed. They lit up all kinds of synapses until hitting the bonus so mother could declare punishment.

"One lawn mowed per dish!"

Going to work on the prize hen, Andrea sealed the end with silly putty taffy'd over wing tips as her thoughts cut to slicing grass heads off five more lawns. She retrofitted Emilio's bicycle pump with a vacuum tube section, sealing the backside to pump in air. Purely for decoration, Andrea pinned on a brown cape borrowed from the back right shoulder of Drewdle's rain slicker. Attached to the hen's side was a Ticonderoga masking as a staff. Pure poutryroticism, the skimpy costume highlighted its brazen nudity.

Safety pins, pulled from mother's junk drawer, tugged at its fatty skin, linked onto fishing line strong enough to haul in a Marlin. Andrea's calculated test weight could easily hold up Fryer Pluck, even with three cups of water sloshing its hollow cavity.

The line had been strung, head at the top of Andrea's ceiling near the window, tail at the hall's end where front door met closet. Taut enough it wasn't noticed, she counted on sag once the launch commenced.

Andrea had thought of Apollonia, Ernestine Hen-in-way, Chicken Courier, Fryer Pluck or Hannah. She was deemed Fryer Pluck after an intense intracranial exercise that AM due to accessorizing ease. Now early PM, the hen's wide open pores bled gelled fat.

Fryer Pluck grew impatient. Her glistening skin slickened, forcing Andrea to wear Drewdle's batting gloves to keep from flopping Fryer to floor. As Andrea stood on her garbage basket flipped onto her desk chair, she held Ms. Pluck in place atop an unbalanced stack of used math textbooks.

She began pumping.

The water, pressed for a place to run, pushed upfront as air forced it forward. Pressured, the water peed through the Silly Putty. Fryer Pluck flew, cannonballing out Andrea's room, the line sagging just enough for door clearance.

Andrea was ecstatic. Fryer Pluck sailed down the hall, safety pins ripping into the buttery flesh as if part of a great Roman tragedy. The cape started fluttering, although not as fantasized, looking more like the spastic beatings of an overweight wren than Vampirella.

Ms. Pluck was well into her first, and final, flight. Andrea's exuberance matching her shiny teeth dulled plaque over enamel. Being a rookie scientist, she hadn't secured the test flight area.

Fryer Pluck glanced off Drewdle's Vitalis-greased melon. The line stretched to accommodate the change in direction, but the change vectored towards mother flying in from the kitchen to see why Drewdle was screaming like a little girl whose Barbie had been buzz cut. Now at a significantly high rate of speed, Fryer Pluck slapped her slimy chest into mother's forehead.

Mother, cold-cocked, was coming to when Andrea's bedroom wall, lacking an anchor bolt, released the line. Fryer Pluck plunged, spilling on mother's exposed midsection, cartilage from Pluck's right wing swabbing out mother's navel. Lightly battered, ready to be fried, a defeated Pluck rolled over, slid off mother and settled on black & white Jackson Pollack'd linoleum.

A Phoenix above the wailing Drewdle gripping his head to keep what little brain left intact, Andrea stood exultantly in the hallway. Fists rose in triumph as she glared at mother while father tried not to tear his abdominals with muted laughter.

Andrea trumpeted her horn of victory.

"Suppress my expression! Suppress my freedom! You can never, ever, suppress my soul!"

August sprung forward, crushing chunks of short-term memory, varnishing long-term. Bush was disappearing in DC under a former 'Nam POW's hard-nosed shadow. The rusty school bell, masquerading as an old rooster who spent countless nights in the henhouse, had been forced into mandatory retirement. As its electronic replacement threw its faux clapper upon faux curves, shoes of various styles, color and disrepair shuffled their way into Mrs. Halverson's 10th grade homeroom.

Stuffed shoes dragged. Teens were greeted by an older unfamiliar student standing next to her desk looking out the window. Between Kristi Kemperhoff and Rusty Merriman, unapologetically overdressed in a Cap'n Crunch colored blouse, a smart tartan skirt and white canvas sneakers, holding four pre-sharpened Ticonderogas, two blue spiral-bound college-ruled notebooks and a tattered copy of Albert Einstein and the Theory of Relativity, stood Andrea Charlene Knowles-Bickerman.

- END -

Steve Rae's formative years were as a professional mud wrestler in rural Nova Scotia. He traveled around the world as a guitar player under the pseudonym "Rocco". He won his wife in a game of pinochle in Buenos Aires Argentina. She is Norwegian.

They have two kids imported from Switzerland. Steve is a self described wonderful composer and guitar player. His best selling album "Songs I thought up myself" set a record for record sales in Saskatoon. Rae is a family name and he is distantly related to Ray Charles whose real name is Rae Charles. Neither of them are French Canadian. Steve spends a great deal of time in USA due to the fact that he accumulated an enormous number of airline miles. When asked about his most proud moment he says "building a log church with a Swiss Army knife for a remote tribe of American Hippies still hiding out in Canada in protest to the Viet Nam war. It required 38 knives to accomplish this. You can see the knives on display at the air strip museum and general store in Waakanoof Indian village in British Columbia.

Bio written by: Tom Grimes

The Wall

The wall echoes the dark clouds and every etched line of the mortar displays a symmetry of marching band correctness.

The Wall stares, daring him to throw the ball. Sweat pops in beads just under the line of golden curls on his forehead. Blue eyes stare through long yellow lashes with as much bravado as a boy of six can muster.

"Not this time," he thinks.

He hikes at the waist like a sailboat on a tight tack, scrunches his innards and throws, aiming at a little notch in the brick that winked at him with inappropriate disdain. He misses the spot and the wall spits the ball back like a cherry seed, but changed. Larger, darker, heavier. Deftly catching it, he transfers from glove to hand and throws in one motion, aiming at the notch but missing again. The wall rifles back another, even larger ball.

His fear drip drips like poison. Blood pulses in his ears.

This six year old's mind can't grasp the malevolence of the Wall. He just wants to play soft toss with a tennis ball but the Wall has different plans.

His fear drips as a heavy dew, of rattlesnake venom. It drips like ghostly eyes.

Every ball he throws returns even larger 'til his panic overfloods its banks. Sweat rivulets down his back, chilling his spine, smelling of porcupine needles.

The boy drags his arm back, glares at the wall compelled by some manic beast to throw again.

The fear nibbles the lining of his intestines. It lingers like bomb struck abbeys. It eats like a cloud of locusts.

And turning, he hurls at the wall hitting the notch.

The wall swallows the ball. Nothing. Then after aching seconds where he can't wrench away his eyes, the Wall with clanking drawbridge chains, opens its hatch and directs the cannon barrel at his puny chest. He clearly sees the smoke belch. All light is extinguished like a black out.

A locomotive sized ball hits him square in the chest pinning him to the grass, squeezing the air from the bellows of his lungs. He pushes with skinny arms but it lies like a dead weight and crushes him. He struggles and thrashes and grass stains his shoulder.

And he screams but no sound comes out as his air is gone. His eyes bulge like overfed rhinos, but the Wall just laughs a gnarly tree laugh. A viper laugh.

At the distant end of the brown dirt drive that snaked in a series of S's, a farmhouse stood like a grain silo on the wheat field prairie. The tallest pines from a long forgotten woodlot had been stripped of greenery and split to planks to build the house. But now like chapped lips the old wood cracked and peeled as the orange of the sun had burned it to grey.

The snow that drifted waist high around the house shimmered silver as the wind blew like waves on the Sahara.

In a tiny bedroom tucked under the eaves, a blonde curly haired boy thrashed under his Dad's old grey army blanket and struggled for breath. Small for his age, he'd been sickly since birth but as in many children such afflicted, a red hot competitive streak stoked his core.

His eyes wild with fever slammed open from the nightmare. Every time he slept, the Wall loomed, taunting him to throw the ball and every time he woke, his dread would increase like a seismic beast in his gullet and his determination would strengthen.

It may have been the drugs to combat the pneumonia that wracked his lungs, but he didn't know or care. He didn't know anything but coughing that torched his chest and left him gasping,

His friends were all outside, playing. Hockey on outdoor rinks that fathers had frozen with midnight watering, gloves freezing on hoses, fingers freezing to gloves. Like all boys who grew up Canadian, it was all he ever wanted to do. But he was too sick. Like a browned out apple core he lay there staring at a yellowed piece of cello-tape left over from a poster his brother had ripped down. Desperate not to sleep.

He was 6 years, two months and 17 days old. He knew because he'd had lots of time to figure it out. He'd been really sick since November and now it was Christmas.

To be a goalie like his hero Terry Sawchuk so goalie pads were what he had asked Santa for, but knew would never get.

"Damnit Irene, when is that boy ever going to get better? We missed summer holidays because of him, now we can't do anything this Christmas either."

In a young boy's vivid imagination he's naughty when his Dad says things like that, so there was no way Santa would bring him what he'd asked for.

But being Christmas morning, still shaking from his nightmare and weak as tepid water he dragged himself from bed chained to his thoughts. Agonized by what had occurred in his sleep he barely noticed the Christmas tree as it faced the living room window.

But stopping short he dropped to his knees because leaning against a red wrapped box was a pair of goalie pads of deep tanned leather with bright white felt backing and leather straps that gleamed with chrome buckles.

And the joy ran like rain. It ran past purple shadows. It ran from drain pipes. It swelled like a river crest at flood tide. He stayed on his knees, shocked that Santa hadn't thought him naughty. Shocked that for the first time in over a month he hadn't thought about breathing.

He finally summoned the courage to touch them, to run his hand over the soft leather, to caress the felt and then to finally strap them on his legs.

The rest of the day passed in obscurity but the feeling of utter joy that flew in the face of fear and sickness has stayed with him.

At the distant end of the brown dirt drive that snaked in a series of S's, the farmhouse still stands like a grain silo on the wheat field prairie. The tallest pines from the long forgotten woodlot stripped of greenery and split to build the house are now covered in beige vinyl.

Now the young boy's face is old and cracked and peeled as the orange of the sun has burned it to red. In the hammock that swings between the porch posts, the old man's droopy eyelids close.

The Wall echoed the dark clouds….

And he still wakes up screaming.

Tom "Tin Cup" Grimes was born in Edmonton Alberta Canada. A gifted grade school student he was give the Inuit name "Chingiinaookanut" which literally translates to "fat little boy who asks too many fucking questions". In the 2nd grade he won the prestigious "Young Canadian School Children of Merit" competition with a powerful essay on how violence in fairy tales impacts childhood sleep patterns and described his own tortured path to self-recovery from recurring nightmares after watching Disney's SnowWhite & the Seven Little People. As Tom quotes "That Dopey is a scary M____F____R!"

Tom's family moved to Texas when he was in the 3rd grade where he earned the scatalogical nom de guerre "Shithead" [Texans really like to engage in scatalogical chit chat]. The nadir of his existence was the 8th grade which he describes as a misasma of hormones, pimples and self loathing. In his HS in the Texas Panhandle he was described as "a purty good ball player" known for his deceptive speed ...
he was even slower than he looked.

After dropping out of college for a 3rd or 4th time Tom spent time in Ireland learning to be a drunk Irish poet but failed at both poetry and debauchery. He does note, with a hint of pride, to being thrown out of a dirty limerick competition in a Dublin bar for being too bawdy ...
apparently the Irish take exception to lyrics that rhyme with douche-bag.

His unbounded literary talent seems only to be eclipsed by his ability to say the wrong thing at the wrong time. Oprah apparently is sensitive about the phrase "How Now Fat Cow" and will have her security thugs drag you from the audience feet first. Tom lives on a small stipend from the families holdings in the colonies. He is married to a former Killer Whale trainer named Christy and has two sons. They are brothers. He still calls Texas home.

"Day at Kinkasan beach"

by Tom Grimes

Ocean deep azure melodies hum beyond the range of hearing,
Sea breezes lick salt grass stands that 'shush' back,
Intermittent bird voices sing sweet high notes,
Surf paints a rhythm of sound as a backdrop,
Clouds whisper hushed ethereal tone poems,
Sunlight plays a jazz riff on the blue water,
It is an unscripted symphony for the eye,
Rousing yet utterly understated,
Perfectly imperfect,
Utterly Osai.

- Timothy Reardon Houston Chronicle art critic commenting on the Wallscape® "Day at Kinkasan beach" by Osai.

The expansive floor to ceiling opticube Wallscape® ran 100 feet in a gentle curve. It was on loan from the Tokyo Museum of Culture. The view was Pacific coastline from a high point on Kinkasan Island. The work spanned a complete day, sunrise to sunset. His professor in Art, Ethics and Technology had given him specific instructions. *"Go, Sit, Experience"*. Leo had been sitting alone in the exact same spot since 5:45 AM. The only distraction a technician dressed in a white jump suit. He didn't stay long.

Wallscape® 3-D imaging required the rare gift of being both artist and mathematician. Most commercial 'scapes' were looping postcards found on walls in dentist offices. Expensive pieces employed encoded optical cube technology making the work unique every time it played. High end 'scapes' were so vivid a winter scene could induce chill bumps. A rare few transcended into the realm of art. This was a sublime masterpiece. Museum literature stated **" ... ,a Zen monk, once meditated on it from sunrise to sunset and wept when night fell ..."**

Osai was famous for injecting humorous twists. Observers reported, on rare occasions, seeing sea monsters suddenly appear and disappear. Despite his rapt solitary vigil the morning had been uneventful … no sea monsters. So here he sat awkwardly cross-legged on a Zafu cushion filled with buckwheat husks. It was 9:45 AM. Soon the museum would be open to the general public. Out of the corner of his eye he saw the technician return and sit down on a bench.

The visitor began scritching about in a brown paper sack. A round object emerged. Leathery hands wielded a small knife. The sweet perfume of summer peaches filled the air ... "Would you like a peach?"

Without looking at the man Leo mumbled *"No thank you"*. His left foot was asleep.

A peach slice went in the mans mouth *"mmm, perfectly ripe, are you sure?"* ... he extended a peach section toward him on the end of his knife.

"No thank you" he muttered as he twisted to look at the man. A round crinkly brown face with dark almond eyes smiled back at him. His back felt out of alignment.

A rich supple voice murmured ... *"Grandfather had a peach orchard when I was a boy"* ... he kept carving the fruit ... *"Early morning, best time to harvest, we would go to the orchard. He would tell funny stories, my favorite was ..."*

Interrupting Leo said *"We need to be quiet"* putting his index finger to his lips. His stomach growled. He craved a caffeine packed venti sized double espresso Starbucks.

***"Why? We're the only ones here."* ... another slice disappeared.**

"I know you are taking your break, but I'm here doing research ... please be respectful."

***"Research? It looks like a hungry young scholar is sitting on a round pillow staring at a wall"* ... the old man grinned mischievously.**

"Did I say I was hungry?" Leo's stiff back grabbed. He wasn't used to sitting on floors for long stretches.

***"Your stomach did, it rumbled 'feed me' "* ... a second impaled slice was proffered.**

"Do you know what this WALL is?" his voice a bit sharper, *"This WALL*

is 'Day at Kinkasan beach' by Osai, Japan's greatest living artist.

The man studied the wall ... *"It looks like a very nice beach."*

"A beach, a beach, is that all you see. It is a masterwork. It's one of a kind ... you can almost smell the ocean".

"Why not go to the ocean instead?"... **he wiped his hands on a red cloth dangling from his back pocket.**

"Don't you know anything about the Osai exhibit?" He waved a glossy booklet at him ... *'Sahara'? 'Nepal Mountain Storm'? Have you never heard of 'Pacific', the largest Wallscape® in the world?*

He studied the wall again ... *"See any sea monsters"?* ... he smiled as he bit, peach juice escaped and fell on his white jump suit. He laughed.

The young man stood up and glared at the old man. *"I got here before dawn to study this 'Wall'. You plop down, gawk like a tourist at the zoo, gobble fruit, and ask about sea monsters. Maybe you need to get back to what you were doing."*

The man was eating a peach. With a nod, he smiled warmly at the young scholar and ambled away ... humming.

Leo was flustered. He didn't intend to be an asshole. But his back had a persistent ache, he was low on caffeine and damn hungry ... spinning he kicked the cushion across the room.

An impeccably dressed museum employee came over. *"Sir, is there a problem?"*

"Yes, I'm UT graduate student here to study the Osai. Your technician"...

pointing toward the retreating figure in white ... "*acted like he was at a zoo. He had no respect, eating peaches, babbling ... he ruined my experience"*

The woman looked at him incredulously *"You don't know who he is?"*

"I don't care if he is the curator of the museum, he was a pest".

"He's not the curator, that's my job, I'm Dr. Elizabeth Cressey," she extended her hand.

Without extending his he flatly stated *"Leo Vondel"*

Dr. Cressey shifted her gaze to the Wallscape® inhaling a slow deep breath then said *"It's incredible"*. She turned and left.

He could hear noises. People were about to come in the hall to gaze at the vast Wallscape®.
He sat down.

The brown paper bag sat on the bench beside him. He fished around and pulled out plump peach. He studied the fruit, feeling its fuzzy skin, inhaling aromas, absorbing color ... then bit deeply ... sweet peach juice squirted onto his shirt. A splashing sound caused him to look back up at the Wallscape®.

He laughed.

When not unleashing Wild Fiction, Blaine Parker is an advertising and voiceover geek, an amateur pizzaiolo, and a brewmaster specializing in top-fermented ales. Formerly a professional yacht racer and stand-up comic (though not simultaneously), he's the author of two books on radio advertising; the co-writer of several screenplays circling various levels of development hell; and winner of many, many incredibly prestigious advertising trophies presently swathed in bubble wrap and stuffed into cardboard boxes in his garage. A Creative Director for a Los Angeles radio network, and voicing radio and TV commercials from coast to coast, Blaine has managed to unplug from the high-voltage residential matrix of Los Angeles' urban desert to cavort atop a mountain in Utah with various elk, moose, scared chipmunks, one unruly black cat, and his much funnier and more talented wife, Honey.

Curiosity At 8,000 Feet

by Blaine Parker

Why did it kill him?
The proverbial him, that is.
Locally and immediately, this specific animal? It wasn't killing him in the least.
He just kept poking his little black nose into everything with an intense desire to *know*.
And why?
Impossible to figure out.
And why was The Wife, a woman preternaturally possessed of nary a single shred of need to know, enamored of this intensely probing, prying hairball? Did it have something to do with the move from the city to the country? The cat was just one of many changes. Other such changes included hawks shopping for lunch outside the window, turkey vultures wheeling above the house in pursuit of anything left by such a hawk, marmots standing up on rocks like little fur-clad jockeys, surveying the landscape, deathly oblivious to the hawks, and families of moose wandering around the property and occasionally looking in the windows. Did curiosity ever kill the moose? Ignorance has certainly cost the marmot. But for some reason—probably alliteration—the cat remains iconic.
"He's so cute."
"He's destroying our furniture."
"It's not that bad."
"My father believed cats belong in the barn."
"We don't have a barn and your father was a supercilious old fart."
Supercilious?
Whatever.
The Wife's curiosity quotient was so low, there was a 99% certainty that if someone left a shoebox full of angry live bees on the kitchen counter, there was no chance she'd get stung. She might notice the buzzing, but wouldn't care enough to look inside. Just so long as the TV volume could drown it out.
That cat, however, needed to know everything.
Taking a shower? There he is, poking his nose through the curtain. Working at the computer? Suddenly, he's on the desk, sniffing the monitor. Fixing a sandwich? He's leaping up to inspect the mayonnaise.
Cute?

Perhaps.
Not cute?
The endless clawing, gnawing, ripping and rending. Upholstery, shoe laces, shoes themselves, clothing—anything capable of happily snagging an extended claw.
Then, of course, there were the rodents.
Chipmunks primarily.
New toy.
Walk through the living room in your bare feet, you'd invariably find one.
Dead of curiosity.
Just not his own.
Incidental feline curiosity.
What happens if I play with this? How long can I play with this? Should I bring this in the house to share with those two large bipedal creatures? Surely, they will enjoy it as much as I.
The worst wasn't the dead chipmunks.
It was the crippled chipmunks.
You only need to see one dragging its useless hind legs around the yard—or the living room—in an effort to elude this ever curious nemesis to remind yourself just how lucky you are to be a biped rather than, say, lunch.
It was also impressive how agile those stricken rodents could be. And the way things were going, it was only a matter of time before we had dozens of paraplegic chipmunks dragging their shattered bodies around the yard like some kind of bizarre outdoor Walter Rodent Reid.
Now, granted, this might not carry the same stigma as if it were happening down in the Ward & June Cleaver lowlands, where the Neighborhood Decency League might knock on our door and ask us to control the furry black curiosity factor.
This is the outskirts of civilization at the edge of indecency. A nice little retreat in a remote mountain subdivision a 20-minute drive and 1,000 feet in elevation from the nearest supermarket. Low real estate prices, scads of nature, and the distinct impression that this is where The Road Ends. Moose and elk for neighbors, along with some hearty, hard partying people who use words like "cornice," "piton" and " Gore-Tex."
These are not people who would begrudge their neighbors a few furry expendables at the paws of a predatory house pet.
Though, it was difficult not to feel for the compact little creatures.
"We really ought to figure out some way to keep him off the chipmunks."
"I don't think that's possible. It would be denying his essential catness."

His essential catness?
Where the hell did that come from?
But, the fact that this curiosity-free woman was suddenly speaking in zen koans was not the essential problem.
No, the essential problem was simply this:
Hate that cat.
And my own curiosity was beginning to bubble.
What would happen if, one day, while out on a chipmunk search & destroy mission, he simply didn't return?
It would certainly be easy enough to blame on his demeanor. "Well, you know how he likes to check things out. Poke your nose in a badger hole, and there are consequences."
But was I really cold enough to make it so?
Each time doubt reared its head, it was placed in check by the sight of a shredded armchair ($699 at the local blow-out boutique), a shredded trail shoe ($89 at the local Gore-Tex emporium), or a clawed LCD TV screen ($1299 at a deep discounting online merchant near you).
This animal was manic.
And expensive.
He was doing more damage than any canine ever could.
He was upsetting the balance of nature outside the door.
He was eviscerating the lifestyle within.
He was a pain in the ass.
Hate that cat.
And somehow, The Wife was unfettered and free from care about this black tornado that was ransacking every possible corner of our existence.
God forbid there should be feet on the coffee table or a crusty cereal bowl in the sink. That could be guaranteed to raise some hackles.
But the plucking pricking pranking prizing of sharp shredding shanking shearing cat claw cacophony merely made her smile as she gingerly scooped the animal from whatever piece of furniture he was improving and stroked him like a prince.
Don't get me started on the litter box.
Maybe I was indeed cold enough.
Could always blame it on the owls.
"You've seen the wingspan on those creatures. They could carry away a pot-bellied pig. Cat? No match. Sorry, hon. How about a dog? Or a long-haired guinea pig. I hear they can even be housebroken."
But.
Could it be done?
And if so, then how?

Finally, an opening.

She had to leave town on business. Several days of just me and the Furry Black Death.

Perhaps a bit of his own scourge could be visited back upon him. Is karma just for people? Why not for domesticated animals?

He was sitting on the arm of the sofa like an Egyptian idol.

He looked at me.

"Meow."

Damn it.

This wasn't going to happen.

He yawned. He stretched. He meowed again. He started clawing the arm of the sofa.

A flick on the ear sent him fleeing.

Things were quiet for a bit.

Until about an hour later.

Walking through the bedroom, that distinctive pulling sound could be heard, muffled, emanating from the walk-in closet. A peek inside revealed Mr. Curiosity improving the left sleeve of a $400 Irish linen sport coat.

My sport coat.

The Irish linen sport coat I was married in.

To a woman who becomes overtly aroused by a man wearing linen.

Not that there's a lot of occasion to wear such a garment up here in the land of Gore-Tex and wild honey.

But damn it, it's still a $400 sport coat that I got married in to a woman who, for some reason, is able to stand having me around.

Seething with something visceral, perhaps even primal (can one be primal about Irish linen?), I swooped down and grabbed him with one hand, resisting the temptation to simply hurl him out the front door. Stalked through the house to the garage. Opened the door, hit the automatic opener and went to the Tool Corner, where various long-handled tools gathered in solidarity against yard work.

A short, olive drab entrenching tool was within easy reach. A good, cat-sized implement. Suitable for both hatchet-like smacking and grave digging. Hefting it in the other hand, I ducked out under the still-opening garage door and made a beeline for the back of the property. Thick with scrub oak, it seemed as good a place as any to do the deed.

The cat, meanwhile, was just along for the ride. He hadn't yet sniffed out ill intent. They say animals can smell fear. Can they also smell homicidal rage?

Perhaps I was not raging enough.

Trudging through the brush and scrub, we reached the edge of the property, the cat and I. He was starting to squirm. Holding him more tightly wasn't helping. And the flaw in the plan (or lack thereof) was beginning to emerge: cat in one hand, collapsed entrenching too in other.

Unfolding the entrenching tool's shovel head required two hands.

Put this animal down, and he's gone.

The animal suddenly began doing what he does best: clawing. And now, he was clawing me. Squeezing him as tightly as possible with one arm, I used the other to grip the entrenching tool (frequently mischaracterized by the layman as a "folding camp shovel") and tried opening it against my foot.

The cat began to hiss and snarl and draw blood not his own.

I used words that cannot be said on television.

Somewhere, a hawk skreeled.

That was it.

Deep within the cat, that sound—that skreeling, visceral, some-small-animal-is-about-to-be-lunch sound—triggered a burst of genetically programmed energy that brought new strength, even more vicious clawing, drew more blood, and finally launched him from my grip and into the brush.

He darted behind a stand of scrub oak with sounds of crunching leaves and frantic feline maneuvering.

The only logical response, of course, was to take chase.

Entrenching tool gripped in one hand, blood dripping from various claw marks, I dashed behind the same stand of scrub oak.

The cat was nowhere to be seen.

But...

The moose calf was.

Uh oh.

The calf made a huffing, guttural noise and clamored in the opposite direction.

Where was…

At the sound of more and bigger crunching behind me, I turned slowly.

There she was.

Mom.

A big cow moose.

An unhappy one.

She wound up her gangly, knock kneed frame and charged.

I turned and ran.

Through the scrub oak and past the house. Across the front yard. Galloping hooves and laboring hairy beast huffing at my heels.

Maybe I could slow her in the Aspens at the edge of the property.

I ran for the trees, and tripped on something.

A blur of brown and green as I roll end over down the hill in front of the house, limbs flailing.
Uncontrolled, the entrenching tool smacks against my face. A sharp, stinging pain sears my forehead and the bridge of my nose. Sharp sticks jab my rolling sack of meat and stupidity as big rocks punch at whatever rolled within reach.
The rolling stops.
The pain throbs.
I look up from the pile of me to the top of the hill.
Looking down is the gangly, knock-kneed cow, apparently satisfied that the threat has been eliminated. She turned and walked away. Her footsteps shuffling through the dirt, disappearing into the afternoon.
I moved.
It hurt.
Bad.
Lying there not moving seemed like a good plan.
I refused to take it as a sign that the turkey vultures were wheeling through the sky above. They were always doing that.
I finally stopped watching the vultures and rolled on my side and into a blanket of pain. It caressed my forehead, nose, shoulder and leg. The entrenching tool lay several feet away, a crimson rivulet along the edge of the blade. That probably explained the sharp pain across my face.
I considered my options. Looking at the interesting angle with which my left leg was pointing, climbing back up didn't seem like the best idea. Maybe I could haul myself back up, hand over hand.
Or, roll down the rest of the way down the hill to the road. Hope someone drives past and recognizes me as something better than road kill.
As I pondered the options and enjoyed the depths of my pain, that special music began playing in my pocket. Under other circumstances, I might dance to it. Reaching around awkwardly, I got my hand into my jeans and pulled out the phone.
"Hey, hon. What's up?"
"Just some time to kill before my flight. Thought I'd call. I miss you already."
"I miss you, too."
"What're you doing?"
"Playing with the cat, of course."
"Really?"
"Yes indeedy."
"You hate that animal. What're you playing?"
"Evasive jungle maneuvers."
"Sounds like fun."

"Oh, it is."
"Don't let him draw blood. No biting."
"Nothing to worry about."
"You OK? You sound funny."
"Just fine."
Meow.
From his perch on a small boulder jutting from the side of the hill, just above my head, the cat was looking down at me.
"Here he is now. Want to say hi?"
Meow.
"Nice to know the two of you are finally getting along."
"It was only a matter of time."
"Well, I'll let you two get back to your fun. Love you."
"Love you."
"Talk to you tomorrow."
"You bet."
Bleep.
I closed the phone.
I supposed I could call someone.
A neighbor.
Someone wearing Gore-Tex who'd know how to use pitons to extract me from my own stupidity.
I looked at the cat.
He was washing himself.
Stupid animal.
Hate that cat.

When Jean left the orphanage, she knew three things about herself. She was a natural entrepreneur, was politically conservative and was going to wring every last adventure out of her dish rag of life. She voted for George Bush and Dick Chaney.....once and named her first business, a brothel, in their honor. The "Bush and Dick Armadillo Ranch" thrived the first few years. As she was sitting bored in the big house, she was reflecting upon her arrest including the towing and impounding of her car. An idea pounced on her brain. She decided to spread her entrepreneurial wings once again and started a new business towing and impounding cars. She appropriately named the business, The Happy Hooker. After "The Accident", she thought she was taken over by a "walk-in" as there was no resemblance to her former self. Her name even changed after she married a geologist. She decided to match her career to her conservative political views and became an accountant. To create some continuity with her former self in the hope of retaining something familiar, she reluctantly created a blog called The Naked Accountant.com in which she uncovers and exposes the tricks of the trade in the mysterious world of money. Jean lives in the Texas Hill Country with her fabulous husband and two Himalayan cats.

The Accident

By Jean Carpenter-Backus

I remember the day my world shattered into a million pieces and my path was forever altered. Driving to work at 7:15am, April 9th, I plunged headlong toward miracles I could never have foreseen.

Bubbling with excitement I enjoyed the spring morning, drinking in the colors of wildflowers that draped the Austin highway like a tapestry. Pale Texas Bluebonnets and orange Indian Paintbrush bloom spectacularly in April and springtime exudes an unmistakable sweetness.

The weather was 70 degrees and foggy with a light drizzle that glistened on the highway. I smiled, thinking, "Six days until the end of tax season!" A tax accountant, I worked brutal hours this time of year and I sensed with palpable excitement through a fog of overwork that I neared the end.

An 8:15am appointment with a client who sold French furniture was to be my last meeting prior to the April 15 deadline. Excited, I told my husband as we got ready for work that after "one last meeting" I'd be able to focus on getting the work out.

I stopped at a little coffee shop. It was new and they'd done a first class job of decorating with tables and chairs where one could sit and read the paper. The double doors swung open and the aroma of roasted beans slapped my face with smile. I made a mental note to come back when I had more time to read the paper over coffee at my leisure.

But not today. Not today.

My latte was ready. I paid, waved goodbye and got back into my car, put the latte in the cup holder, started the engine and resumed my thirty-minute journey to the office. Favorite music playing in the background, I chose the scenic route to work. Although this was a path I rarely took, I chose it because it wrapped around a beautiful subdivision and golf course. The tricky part would be crossing Southwest Parkway. Yesterday's two-lane country road was now a four-lane super-highway.

Springtime. New life.

I stopped at the stop sign, looked both ways and crossed Southwest Parkway listening to music and sipping my latte. I would arrive at the office a little ahead of my 8:15 appointment. I never saw the convertible Sebring doing seventy miles per hour. They tell me it was white.

My husband Andrew remembers hearing the radio report about a serious accident on Southwest Parkway. He said a silent prayer for those involved but didn't give it any more thought since he didn't know anyone who traveled that route. Driving blithely to work, he was shocked when his phone jangled unexpectedly.

It was my assistant, Chris. "Andrew, have you seen Jean? Her 8:15 has been here for nearly fifteen minutes. And you know Jean's never late without calling." In a moment of clarity Andrew remembered I had left around 7:15 and that I was completely focused on my 8:15 "last" appointment. "Have you checked with the hospitals?" he asked.

Where the heck had that thought come from?

Chris laughed with gallows laughter. "No…the phones have been ringing off of the hook."

"Well, maybe she got hung up at a coffee shop or stuck in traffic. I'm sure she'll be there soon."

They got off the phone and Andrew continued driving to San Antonio. He tried calling my cell phone but kept getting only voice mail. It made no sense. The more he thought about it, the more he knew something was wrong.

"There's no way Jean would be 15 minutes late for that meeting without calling the office with an explanation." Voice mail again.

He pulled over to the side of the road, his heart beating rapidly. He called Chris, "Has Jean shown up yet?"

"No, and the clients are annoyed,"

"Have you checked with any hospitals?"

"Never crossed my mind. But I've tried her cell phone and it just goes to voice mail."

Andrew realized Chris wasn't picking up on his level of concern due to being buried in the thick of tax season. His next call was to the Austin police department. They asked him for the VIN number of my car, as if anyone carries their spouse's VIN number with them! After calling our insurance company and getting the VIN number for the wrong vehicle, one of the police operators took pity on him and said accident victims are generally taking to Brackenridge Hospital.

Andrew phoned Brackenridge and said he was trying to find his wife, Jean Backus, who hadn't shown up for work. He was put on hold until a woman came on the line and said, "I'm a social worker at the hospital, and I understand you're looking for Jean Backus. To whom am I speaking?"

In that instant, Andrew knew I was there. His final hope was that she would tell him my injuries were minor and that all this was just silly red tape.

She said I was there, that I had been in a serious accident and was in intensive care but was conscious and was asking for him. Andrew headed for the hospital.

The Sebring T-boned my Camry in the passenger-side and the front seat reduced to one third its width.

My hips went left as my head and upper body whipped to the right. My head was traveling 70mph toward the passenger side of my car, certain to be cracked open like a watermelon falling off a truck.

If there's such a thing as a guardian angel, mine understood the changing geometry of collapsing steel, opposing forces, flying glass and flying objects. The passenger seat headrest altered the trajectory of my head and kept it from hitting the passenger doorpost. My head slammed instead into the shoulder belt bracket, but at a reduced speed due to the intervention of the headrest. The impact was severe enough to leave part of my scalp in the seatbelt harness and give me a brain contusion on the right side of my head. My brain bounced around inside my skull enough to cause internal bleeding and an injury to my brainstem as well.

Unconscious, my right foot hit the gas pedal and shot my car toward a vacant lot on the far side of the highway, giving me a second chance to die. There was a 35-foot cliff at the back of the lot and little to stop me from tumbling down it.

Luckily, as my car sped across rough ground my foot slipped off the accelerator and my car was stopped by a thick shrub barely five feet from cliff's edge.

The bottom of my Styrofoam latte cup remained in the console, neatly severed from the upper half, its foamy contents splashed across the windshield. My car was half its former width. A passenger would have been instantly crushed.

When the police arrived, they studied the scene and scratched their heads. "What's that Camry doing on top the hill in that vacant lot?"

The white Sebring convertible had spun 90-degrees and run into a Suburban that was stopped on the other side of the intersection. The Sebring's front end was crashed, but the Suburban was barely scratched. It appeared the Sebring and the Suburban had hit head-on.

"What's that Camry doing on top the hill in that vacant lot?"

I drive through that intersection today and feel nothing. *Nothing*. I try to remember *anything* as I drive through it now. It seems strange to me that I should feel so little in the place where I nearly died, the place where my life was forever transformed.

I was lucky. My entire central nervous system was rearranged and my neural pathways were disrupted. They told me later that my short-term memory and balance were completely wiped out. I know also that my anger, hate and negativity were surgically excised from mind and soul. Into the void where they'd been rushed feelings of pure love, wisdom, joy, and a childlike, playful essence. I couldn't conjure a negative thought! Not one.

You might be tempted to think it was the drugs. And that might explain what happened early on. But it doesn't explain the *persistence* of this profound state after every trace of medication had long faded away.

People who visited me in the hospital later told me they expected me to be daffy and watched for "brain injury" signs. You know the ones. They expected my words to slur or my mouth to drool. What they got instead was a new, improved me! All I remember is feeling angelic and loving.

Have you ever been with a good friend and felt like you had to hurry your stories because there just didn't seem to be enough time? I've had those conversations more often than I care to remember. But true friendship takes the time, whatever time it takes, and *makes* that precious time *quality* time.

Quality time with love poured into the mix makes a big difference. Time sings as it flies because there's nothing in the world you'd rather be doing. It's the perfect moment, a defining moment. Something you never forget.

I'm not saying I changed anyone's life while I was in the hospital other than my own. But at every moment I felt present, filled with genuine interest and unconditional love. It seemed as though God came to the hospital, scooped me up, took me to heaven, taught me about love, then gently placed me back into my life in Austin, Texas, and said, "Now go *be*."

We're not supposed to remember these things and I wouldn't claim it for the longest time. "I was brain injured," I'd say to myself. "For crying out loud, stop trying to give that period of time some sort of special meaning! You were brain injured and, well, a little nutty. So stop it and move on."

That's what I said and tried to believe. For ten years. Until now.

My neurologist told me that most people are either physically, emotionally or financially devastated by the injuries I had. Most suffer deeply in permanently debilitating, painful situations for the rest of their lives.

I went somewhere a little different. I went into euphoria. I'm certainly not the only person ever to go into euphoria after a brain injury. Other cases have been documented, but we're so few that the medical professionals really didn't know what to do with me.

I'll admit it took me a decade to put all the pieces together. But now I see clearly and want to share what I discovered with others.

The key that unlocked the truth of my story and the healing I experienced is: *It all has to start… with love.*

"Welcome to the world of words," whispered a voice in her head. Unheeding the interruption, Becca relentlessly plunged onward into the swamp of definitions, complicated words, and narrating. From watching her parent authors frantically type for months at a time, Becca gathered as much information as she could about how to concoct tales and spin stories. From the moment her pencil touched the paper, she never stopped writing. During school, during free time, and even when she was supposed to be doing chores, Becca kept writing. She learned and discarded, remembered and forgot. But she continues to try her best to create wondrous fables every time.

At sixteen, Becca is a junior in high school, and currently keeps herself busy in Fort Wayne, Indiana, living with her parents, John and Jennifer Kaufeld; her brothers, Joe and Isaac, and her parakeets, Skye and Neon. Look for more of her work at *eclectictale.diaryland.com*.

Waiting for *You*

-Becca Kaufeld

As I pass through the shadows, I wait for you. As I pass through the daylight, I wait for you. You know I'm here, but you pretend I'm invisible. You don't want to talk to me, because you might start seeing. You might start noticing other people who need your help to get out. They captured our minds, and they're killing us. Slowly. I've seen the others like me. They're scared, too. We might never make it out, never be free. Please, free us.

Every day, the walls get closer. We're desperate. We don't want to succumb, but we have no choice. They hem us in, forcing us to conform. You haven't seen everything I have. You haven't spent hours listening and trying to make them happy. They never are.

You don't believe. You don't want to help. But it's all true. You call them teachers. I call them jailers, or worse. Are we doomed to die from the start? Please get us out.

They told us, "You have so much potential." They said, "Oh, you'll do well." Well, they were right. We did do well. We didn't believe it either. That's how I know you don't understand

They'll get you too. Who will save us then?

exclusively on
M-G-M
Hank Williams
and Indiana

Taunek-aug

by John Davis

The sight of Santa skinny-dipping in the river was so disturbing - no one noticed. He splashed and treated himself to a brief taste of jolly fun. The Wisconsin River current was just swift enough to carry cool aeration as it swirled around gigantic granite boulders. Santa lowered himself like a hippo, letting long-travelled waters rinse through his curly hair and beard.

Reclining to dry pale pink skin on a slab of sun-warmed stone, he looked up and admired the canopy of leaves lining the riverbank. Today, the world was green. Soaking moments of sunshine, Santa knew it was time. Quickly dressing, he popped open the top of his pocket watch. The image of his bride Elizabeth beamed at him and he smiled back. The watch pulsed in his palm; reminding him of his job and the pressure of being in time.

Above the chorus of river rapids below, Santa heard the wives of Taunek-aug bickering. He foresaw the pain of this family being pushed westward against their will. His friend resisted change. President Buchanan resisted. Every son of the south resisted, but war was coming. Taunek-aug would not hold against it.

Stepping loudly and taking occasion to peck his walking stick against nearby stones, Santa announced his arrival. By the time he came within sight of the wigwam, the image of productive serenity greeted him. Taunek-aug sat cross-legged, face to the sun, and upright back perpendicular to the river. His ebony hair was braided back to reveal three white crane feathers perched behind his right ear. In throne-like fashion, his hands rested on two red granite skull shaped stones.

Taunek-aug's wives labored quietly now. Bright Eyes was sewing a coat of beaver pelts. Winter Sun knelt beside a cook pot. Her knife diced bits of smoked turkey into a broth whose garlic aroma pronounced supper would be especially tasty. Little Thunders stood proud with arms extended palms up in formal greeting, as though this was the first visit. Her voice was clear and firm, "Boozhoo!"

Santa waved, winked, and bowed in greeting, politely

acknowledging Little Thunder's status and her responsibility over the camp. In doing so, three small wrapped gifts fell from the sack he carried on his shoulder. Formality aside, Little Thunder smiled as she reached up to clutch a small silver cross hanging around her neck. Santa remembered when she wished for it the year she chose to become "enamiad", taking on the responsibility of prayer for others.

Taunek-aug petted his stones from right to left and stood without visible effort. Only the wrinkled skin around his eyes betrayed his age. His stature mirrored a young man ready to run a race, accomplish a hunt, or lead a war party. He moved only slightly slower than his smile to embrace Santa in a silent hug. Following their custom, they quietly settled onto individual mats prepared for this occasion. With a deep balance of calm awareness, they each considered the other. Soon many things were obvious, though unspoken.

"Neebing?" Taunek-aug's voice questioned. Santa always found Taunek-aug's voice to be slightly higher pitched than he remembered. "Yes," he replied, "summer fades. The son of the white trapper calls me in my dreams, wishing for strong books of learning. His insight grows quickly."

"Enh-enh," Taunek-aug agreed, once again stroking the stones.

"Do the red stones speak?" Santa prodded.

Taunek-aug used his large leathery hands to cradle the first stone. He drew it up to his lips and breathed deeply. "Mudjimushkeeki gakAbishe." His facial expression was one of anguish and anger. He returned the stone to its place and then touched the other stone in silent respect. Taunek-aug carefully adjusted each, rubbing away bits of earth. "Idam booch babaa-ayaa bangisimonong."

"Enh," Santa nodded in agreement and pointed. "Very bad medicine to the East and South. The sound of war drums. The stones agree. You must travel west, my friend. You have no need of something to guide you, but I give this." Reaching into a deep pocket, Santa presented Taunek-aug a compass, which was acknowledged and placed on the mat. Calm words did not last.

"MigAdinaniwan baataaziwin!" Taunek-aug rose quickly, lifted a walking stick high overhead and back down, beat the ground three times, and snapped the staff into two pieces. Letting out a scream of despair, he tossed them backwards over his head into the river.

Santa spoke softly. “War is not in the earth but in the heart, uprooting all in its path. In time, men forget the blood of violence. Grinding other men into dust, they find themselves in the lifeless eyes of their foe.”

A brown bear lumbered into sight and crossed the river, causing a mighty swirl through the gurgling current. Santa glanced at his pocket watch. Satisfied, he then picked up a rock and threw it playfully at the creature while chuckling under his breath. “He wants to be a banker. What freedom is in that?”

By the time Bently lumbered his soaked hide out of the river, he had snagged a large muskellunge in his mouth. Shaking himself too close to where Winter Sun was cooking, she squinted her eyes at him. Ignoring her anger, he shuffled over to drop the fish. “For the stew,” Bently mumbled gruffly as he chose a seat of flat stone. Both Santa and Taunek-aug watched as the mammoth creature yawned, fish guts dripping from his teeth. In open disgust, Winter Sun threw the fish back into the river.

“You don’t belong here. I told you to stay north.” Santa scolded with a smile.

“Enough! Change me back. Being a bear is not what I intended. Solitude follows freedom closer than a gander follows a goose.”

“Very well. But choose with more thought. Do you want the life you asked to leave behind? Are you so quick to trade freedom and dominance for a pair of polished boots and a top hat of beaver felt? As I’ve told you before, you can live the life you wish. Be happy.”

Bently stood on hind legs and growled as he demanded, “I want to be a man again!”

Santa reached in his bag and drew out a ring of keys. Shaking his head, he tossed them towards Bently, who caught them with a five-fingered hand. “Liberty is an illusion pursued by those who lack vision. You seek power over others but will find others who have dominion. Now go ask Bright Eyes for something to put on.”

Taunek-aug cradled a stone in each palm. Standing, he searched upstream. **“Jeemonnug.”**

Santa walked to the brink of the riverbank and studied the movement of the hands on his watch. A canoe came into view and he stepped into the water, relishing the coolness flowing between his toes. Grabbing the stitched wooden stern pushed the bow around downstream, but Santa held fast. Behind the cargo of pelts, a smile peeped through a bushy beard. "You are an unexpected sight, old man." The trapper stepped out of the boat and helped Santa lug the canoe to dry ground.

With familiarity known to those who wander, introductions and reunions were accomplished. Taunek-aug took his role as host and beckoned his wives to serve food to his guests. Soon, this peculiar group of seven sat in a circle enjoying turkey stew from small wooden bowls.

Bently placed his bowl on the ground in front of him and ate bear fashion. The beaver coat on his back gave the illusion of a shaggy dog cowering over his stolen part of a family meal. The others more politely used their fingers and pieces of bread to eat the stew. Bently was done first and began his story. "It's a very big world I've been traveling! I'm damn glad to be human again. When it comes to being civil and living lives of brotherly love, men are on top. I've seen animal brutality that would make the strongest man faint." Bently stood and walked over to the cook pot. Without pausing, he dropped his bowl and took the pot.

Looking back at the group, Santa spoke. "Daniel, your canoe is not full. Why return now?"

"No choice. The beaver are mostly gone. I've decided to pack the family and move to Missouri. When the fur buyers come north, I'll have the cash for..."

"Go further, Southeast!," Bently interrupted. "Southern ladies and gentlemen have reached the pinnacle of civilization. Me, I'm heading for Georgia to enjoy all the comforts of Dixie."

Trunek-aug's hands began to tremble as he worried one of his precious stones. His eyes remained closed. Noticing, Santa consulted his watch again, sadly shaking his head at the talent some men have to make really bad decisions.

"Daniel, I've brought some books for your son. Take them to him and give my love to the family."

"Certainly and thank you! I'm anxious to get home. Matilda

and the baby were not well when I left." Daniel looked to the sky. Bently wandered back over, wiping his dripping mouth on his arm, and settled into the canoe. "Mind if I ride along?"

Santa rolled his eyes and slipped a coin into Daniel's hand. "Buy him some clothes." He gave the canoe a push. Even though the canoe quickly passed from sight, he continued to hold his right hand up in salute, eyes moist as he whispered a final good-bye.

Taunek-aug toppled both of the stones. His eyes were wide as he searched for reason to explain the pain and sorrow he had foreseen in the lives of the men who floated away. He pointed back to the mats. The two friends once again sat in silence. As in their greeting, they now searched for understanding and hope needed for a proper parting.

Little Thunders came and stood beside Santa. In her hand she held a pouch of freshly picked berries. In the silent space between the ticking of his watch, he found the magic of unborn life in Little Thunder. Taunek-aug would have a daughter in the Spring. He gave her a tremendous hug as he kissed her hair. "You are the river! Be happy. Be free!" He added the berries to his bag as she pirouetted towards her home in response.

Taunek-aug raised both stones above his bowed head. A sad tune came from his throat that resonated through his head and filled the air. His feet shuffled in a dance of parting.

"Anâwâbama - - - gichi-inakamigad, ijinad nibôwin - nishiwanâdakamigad enigokwag." Tearful eyes opened to see his friend in smiling conflict to his discouraging song of death, disease, trouble and pain.

Santa knelt at the river bank. Dipping his hands, he scooped a refreshing drink. He splashed his face and slicked back his white hair and beard. With lifted arms and hands exploding into fingers that pointed fiercely at the sky, Santa yelled: "Kagige bimâdisiwin nongom. Life everlasting today. Nin sâgiidimin. We love one another! - - - Nin bosakâgon. - - - nogorn! Today - - - nogorn!"

With a quick glance at his watch, Santa announced, "It is my time to return home. It is your time to travel to a new one. My friend, there is still much to love and live if you stay ahead of the war drums." Looking at the rocks, he continued. "They cry out in pain. There will be much bloodshed here before the snow comes." He hugged Taunek-aug tightly, picked up his sack, and skipped away North to the last leafy tree before all others were pine, spruce, and fir. He laid a finger along side of his nose and giving a nod, he paused, admiring the ticking of his timepiece. At precisely 10:10, Santa closed his watch and was out of time.

Taunek-aug sat beneath the stars with the summer moon peeking above the top of Rib Mountain. His red stones were at his side moaning the memory of ancestral roots. But tonight, Taunek-aug splashed his toes in the river dreaming of life in a new land. From the wigwam, Little Thunder began to sing.

© BAIN

The ever shy Darby Young lives in a town near the middle of the country that does not boast a Starbucks, much to her dismay. She's been a struggling book addict since age seven or so, and upon occasion, can be seen 101 miles away from her house at the nearest Barnes and Noble. Other than reading, she enjoys learning the Craft of War with her dearest elven friends, spending time in a companionable state of laughing hysterics with her family and traveling both beyond and within the confines of the physical world.

THE BETRAYER.

by Darby Young

Wild grass swayed as a gentle breeze kissed its sun touched leaves. His heart was breaking. He wept bitterly for the wrongs he was about to commit, thoughts spinning like a maelstrom of emotion, seeking the one thing he could never have: acceptance. He prepared to battle the one man who could give him that, to battle his own nation, the nation he loved. For the sake of love, he would destroy it.

It was time they knew. The life he led, the friends he had forsaken, his pain. They would know the lies of their king. The king would feel his pain. The king would feel the loneliness of being unwanted…the powerful, sickening rage…the bitter sadness, when all hope and happiness was taken from him. The king would pay for his crimes against him.

He would never escape the hell he was about to unleash on the world. His life was over. No longer his mother's pet and tool, no longer the bane and one regret of his father's life. He was no longer himself, the gentle knight. No one could tame the animal he had become. They were right. He was a mongrel, a bastard child, demon child, unfit to live. He was to prove it to them in the cruelest way. The memory of his betrayal would never fade. The image of the king, lying, blood on his crown in a field of dead compatriots, would never fade.

He wanted a swift end to all. He fought the battle and watched all the foolish men who trusted him die. He fought his father, the man he loved and admired. He was younger, stronger. He would watch his father die at his own hand. Everything was over. The world, ending; the sky falling into shadow.

The stained grass swayed and danced mournfully in the blood-red sunset as the betrayer left, shedding tears for his fallen enemy.

MARGARET TITUS WAS BORN IN THOMASVILLE, GEORGIA IN 1948. AFTER ATTENDING LOYOLA UNIVERSITY IN NEW ORLEANS, LOUISIANA, SHE RETURNED TO THOMASVILLE. SHE HAS BUILT A SUCCESSFUL BUSINESS WHILE RAISING FOUR CHILDREN, PRIMARILY AS A SINGLE MOTHER. ON MOONLIT NIGHTS, SHE CAN BE FOUND TEARING UP THE STREETS OF THIS RURAL HAMLET IN HER BLACK, CONVERTIBLE ROADSTER.

And We Thank You For it All

The massive old oak was the biggest tree on the block, growing in the wrong place, much too close to the road and right in the path of the utility cables. Its gnarled limbs draped and sagged under hoary grey beards of Spanish moss that constantly dropped into my yard and tangled around the power lines. And because it grew where a front drive might have been, visitors were forced to parallel park on the narrow city street. In short, it was a nuisance. But it had lived in that spot for over a hundred years-much longer than the low brick houses and Styrofoam doctors' offices that surrounded it. To me that granted it a certain entitlement that oddly calmed my harried soul. And its broad evergreen umbrella shaded us from the merciless South Georgia sun, so I loved itanyway. Even my fastidious neighbor deferred to it in spite of its kite-like leaves darting and diving into his immaculate lawn and crashing into his square headed, crew cut shrubs.

Throughout the earth cracking dry months, I nurtured the old tree with constant care. Day in and day out, IVs of water dripped from a soaker hose encircling its base, quenching the deep thirst of roots trespassing under my neighbor's driveway and beneath the steaming asphalt street. Years back, the man from Bartlett's Tree Service had frowned disapprovingly at the ivy thriving in the tree's upper branches. "Bad for the tree." he had scolded. "Saps its vigor and stresses it-makes it vulnerable to disease."

So, like a dutiful nurse, I pruned and re-pruned the parasitic vines from its trunk and pulled them off as high up as I could reach. Severed from the sustenance of the soil, they should have died, but they didn't. Greedy for life, they groped and sucked their way toward the heavens, indifferent to their unresisting host.

Tending the old tree was easy, even therapeutic, compared to deciphering the needs of my aging parents. Daddy had been sick most of the last two years. Seven kids, sixty seven years of marriage and a long stint in the Georgia legislature had worn his soldierly, World War Two determination down to stoic acceptance of just about anything life threw his way. The worst thing lately had been my Mother's stroke. He wouldn't set boundaries, or guard his own space even if it meant exhausting himself to the point of illness. Married at 18 and 21, their joined- at- the- hip life cost him dearly when she could no longer walk or speak. Before that he had weathered the blitzkrieg of raising seven wild and at times downright bad kids, hanging on until we fulfilled our protracted adolescence and miraculously metamorphosed into creative adults. "Takes a long time to grow up" he reminded me when I whined to him about my own kids' foolishness. It was alright with him if his children, grandchildren and even great grandchildren needed to crash and burn a few times on their yellow brick roads to authentic lives. "Just keep the faith with 'em 'till they come around, you can't change 'em, they got to change themselves. I'll be praying for 'em." And he did, closing each conversation with his fatherly God with simple words of gratitude, "And we thank you for it all."

He was a story teller-with over a thousand articles written like letters from a friend for his beloved Sunday nature column in the local newspaper. Humming birds, hawks, gardenias and gator fleas were equally worthy of his respectful attention and unique literary voice. After over a half century lived in his quirky old house in the middle of a pristine forest prime evil he had become one with his wild community. Clearly his heart's home was more outside than in. He knew each fox, its mate and kits. He spoke the language of owls, and enjoyed a personal friendship with Mr. Green, a tiny frog who lived in his shower, delighting his grandchildren and terrorizing the occasional guest. He seemed to tolerate the aggravations and idiosyncrasies of the house by being just as cantankerous as it was. Like very old friends fully aware of each other's annoying flaws but long past trying to change them, they had made their peace.

"Dad you've got to get some rest." I cajoled, "take some time for yourself and let go of all the problems with this old house. You should move out of these woods into town to a nice new assisted living apartment. Mom could enjoy the activities she likes and you could have some quiet time to yourself." I reasoned.

"I'll leave Cedar Run feet first." he stated flatly. Logic was irrelevant. And so he sat, an old monk in a Lazy Boy, contemplating his woods--and as usual, he was right. Eventually he was taken by ambulance to the hospital-"feet first."

Fay made her entrance in sheep's clothing, no big deal, not a hurricane, just a tropical storm-and we desperately needed the rain after a scorching summer drought. She began her binge in Florida--staggering and stumbling across the peninsula like a drunken fool crashing through a crowded bar. She lurched and swayed her slow way north-reeling from coast to coast and back again. Finally she collapsed unconscious against South Georgia and heaved her bile on a landscape ill prepared for such wanton weather. Gushing and raging she turned streets into rivers and parks into lakes. Suburban lawns croaked and slithered with creatures meant for swamps and ponds-and still she spewed her crazy torrents. Beneath waterlogged canopies ancient trees swooned as their venerable roots lost their grip on the spongy loam that had nurtured them for centuries.

Inside the hospital I sat in silence at my father's side--the relentless sickness driving him down with each clap of thunder. His young but old fashioned physician gently confirmed, "He cannot get well. All the tests are clear." We knew his wishes-put down in plain English. No heroics-no exceptions! I sat watching him as a new mother watches her sleeping infant. With time expanding between each tired breath, I swallowed a flood of tears and a lifetime of love to speak final words of tenderness and gratitude to this giant who was slipping his Earthly roots--roots that had held him and his family upright for 88 years.

Returning home through the howling downpour, surreal feelings swirled my brain into a bitter parfait of confusion and anger. How could he be gone? How absurd for life to go on with business as usual. His entire existence had been a sacrament of reverence for the creation. Surely the planet must take note of his passing--something important should happen to mark his leaving!

Outside, sewers gurgled and choked, frantically emptying their unspeakables onto city streets, while inside, my roof thumped with the dissonant rhythm of hard green pine cones hurling themselves prematurely from slender branches. Numb and exhausted, I curled myself into my bed and stopped-stopped thinking, stopped feeling and stopped hurting. Through the chattering chaos a muffled thud jerked the foundations of my house and light left the streets. Utter blackness oozed over the night as sleep swaddled me in a blanket of nothingness.

Morning didn't dawn. It fumbled and slopped its way through the soggy stench of Fay's throbbing hangover. Her dissipation complete, remorseless, she blithely left.

I awoke to an alien inner voice telling me Daddy was gone and I was still here. Looking around my home of 16 years, everything was the same yet nothing felt familiar. Objects I had seen a thousand times were naked and exposed, in need of justification for their being. My great grandmother still watched in regal silence from the family photo gallery. The skylight still misted the dim hallway with pastel light. And the soft sounds of my newborn granddaughter's sleep still murmured from the guest room. My five senses told me nothing had changed, yet some other sense more undeniable than sight or sound knew that something fundamental had twisted, and things I had taken for granted yesterday were weirdly out ofcontext today.

Drifting aimlessly from room to room I stared dumbly out my window at a world ransacked by water and wind. Power lines dragged their ugly black tentacles through my boxwood hedge. In the distance, radios barked out clipped orders in staccato voices while eerie red strobe lights pulsed insistent warnings to no one in particular.

Next door my neighbor moved methodically, stacking chain sawed limbs in identical neat rows along the street. Instinctively my eyes moved upward searching the sky for the familiar comfort of the old Oak's towering silhouette. My blood turned to glass and shattered inside my veins! Where leaves and branches should have been, glaring back at me was a gapping grey emptiness and lying pitifully mangled at its feet, the big tree's heart lay broken and splintered, ripped out in the storm.

As a thousand years slipped through a sieve, eternity spread out in my consciousness like oil on a wound, melting me into the universe while the jagged pieces of my heart flew together, magnetized by an unspeakable mystery. Outside of time and thought, I knew what my father had always known--the Creation did know him, knew him still, and knows us all! It is all intended, all known and all good. Each coming, each going, each acorn, each raindrop, each firefly, each fern, each spider, sparrow, rosebud and rock-- loved, valued and indispensable in the perfection he cherished so tenderly.

As the knowing rose up in my chest, pain, like a frightened deer, bolted from its hidden place deep in my gut and leaped into the light of my awareness. The aching, the longing, the remembering, rushed in a swollen river of grief, swirling me helplessly downstream in its cleansing rapids, breaking open my resistance upon rocks worn smooth by eons of flowing life. Yielded, I tasted the sweet salt flavor of acceptance as Grace whispered in a peaceful, beloved voice, "And we thank you for it all."

The Crash

by Bryce McNally

"Please listen to the stewardess and get ready for a fast, and flawless ride." said the captain nonchalantly. "Why do we need to listen to this crap?" I said to the guy next to me, "I mean really, what kind of person doesn't know how to buckle and unbuckle their seatbelt?"

Soon after we took off, the captain turned off the seatbelt sign. I sat quietly as the ladies came up and down the aisles to serve food and drink.
"We are coming up on some light turbulence, but we will be out in about two minutes." Said the captain calmly. But it wouldn't be calm for long. About three minutes later the pilot said that things would be a bit bumpy for the remainder, boy was he right. It got bumpy, then bumpier, after that people started to wonder what was going on. It felt like we were bread crumbs in a shake and bake bag, as he captain said. "We have run into a tropical storm, and have been scheduled to land early." But unbeknownst to him we would only be making one stop along the way. Just then the plane started to lose altitude rapidly. Thoughts started racing through my head like, why didn't I listen to her? How do I get air? How to I use the seat raft? Why didn't I listen to her! Why?

While the plane was careening out of the sky, someone looking up at us could picture a Tylenol falling out of a pill bottle. My mind pacing, my heart racing, and all of my nerves shocked so I couldn't move a muscle. I knew it was over, and then I heard "Don't panic, we are doing all we can do to keep this plane airborne. Remember don't be alarmed, everything will be ok. Wait, what am I saying, we are all going to die. Say your last prayers, because we wont make it out alive."

I thought to myself, why me, why now? What will happen to my family? They were innocent right, why do they deserve my death?
And with that thought, we crashed right into a small strip of highway, crashing into cars and causing turmoil in the lives of everyone around. Why should they have to pay?

After the plane stopped skidding, we found that not many people made it. It was the most excruciating pain I had ever felt. Odd thing was that it was more of a sick pain than a physical pain. I had felt pain for everyone around me and their lives. After I regained selfishness, I looked at myself and realized that I had cuts and bruises all over my body. After seeing my own bodily damage, I passed out. The rescue team showed up about a half an hour later, and retrieved fifteen of the twenty people on the plane, half of them had passed. That was three years ago today.

Adam Donmoyer Bio (Written by Tom grimes)

Adam Donmoyer, real name Adam Popsicle Jones, is a professional political speechwriter and unpaid consultant to the Plaid Textile PAC. He worked as a minor league Super Hero and baseball announcer in a mid sized mid western city for a couple of years until he hurt his back lifting a compact car out of a muddy ditch (not covered in his HMO). Disability is no longer a word in Adam's life however, he told her it was time to move on and left her in a one-bedroom condo in Hoboken, he's never looked back. His work as an understudy in the Barnum & Bailey clown troupe gave him a keen awareness of human tragedy and he now devotes a great deal of time to volunteer to help reformed strip club performers ... in his spare time. He has a lot of spare time. Writing has always been a passion of Adam's, as is weedeating. He currently spends his nights playing piano in non-alcoholic bars (he asked that we not go there.) Adam's personal hero is Mr. Rogers "I love a man who loves sweaters and slippers.

Lunatic

Music and Lyrics by Adam Donmoyer

I'm lying in my hospital bed
There's an IV in my arm
They tell me that I'm lucky
I could've done real harm
I don't believe in Jesus Christ
'Cause I never knew the man
But when I forget to take my pills
I think that's who I am

Jesus Christ, I'm Jesus Christ
And I'm the Son of God
And I can walk on water
I can heal the sick
I can feed the hungry
The truth is, I'm a lunatic

The last time that I lost my mind
I gave a man my car
I fed a hungry family
Maxed out my credit cards
Turned my house into a shelter
For the ones who need a home
They found me at the bank
Jesus, trying to get a loan

Jesus Christ, I'm Jesus Christ
And I'm the Son of God
And I can walk on water
I can heal the sick
I can feed the hungry
When I am a lunatic

My son, he doesn't visit me
He doesn't understand
My only living family
Ashamed of his old man
So when I leave the hospital
If I neglect to take my pills
It's because reality's too hurtful
And I'd rather do God's will
'Cause

Jesus Christ, I'm Jesus Christ
And I'm the Son of God
And I can walk on water
I can heal the sick
I can feed the hungry

Am I such a lunatic?

Adam Donmoyer - Piano, Vocals

Peter Nevland had no idea what he was getting himselfinto when he left behind his engineering job at Motorola in September,2002, to follow his dreams on a road called Spoken Groove. He had norecord deal or name recognition, but he had Paul Finley, a struggling Catholic guitarist who calls his guitar "Mary." He startedperforming for any audience who would listen, giving him front row seatsto stories exploding with witty comedy, perseverance through struggle,and compassion for the outcasts of society.

Peter loves stories. He loves telling them and hearing them. He's performed on countless toursacross the U.S., Canada, England, Germany & Australia, connectingwith just about every audience imaginable. He hasn'tfound an ethnic group or cultural segment whose hearts are toodifferent to be mesmerized by passion about what's important to them."After all, why do we need to have all the right qualifications topursue our dreams?" he asks.

Peter currently balances performances all over the world of his one-man show, "Life with Sort-of Red Hair", conducting creative writing workshops with young people of all ages and consulting business clients as a Wizard of Ads partner. He's a regular contributor to beneaththecover.com, americansmallbusiness.com and his own websites, spokengroove.com and thelandofnev.com. He still has no idea what he's gotten himself into, but he likes it that way.

"Ruhamah"

You were a whore when I met you, Ruhamah. You stood on the side of the road with that old, worn out grin, handled skin, amphetamine-induced sickly levity leering through my jeans to the content of my back pocket. One hand rested slightly above your ill-fitting halter top, stroking your breast, that lewd gesture meant to impress my pupils, suggest the completion of a fantasy not meant for me. Every scent of you reeked of use and abused virtue, misused beauty, refused worth, repulsive, disgusting, and annoying.

I wanted to get away. I wanted to help and heal. But it wasn't pity that led me to woo.
Love drew your heart on mine, an unlikely design to the mind. I called you by your name, Ruhamah. You wanted to be young, Ruhamah. You were clean and new and pure and wholly my bride, Ruhamah.

I didn't lie when I promised to love you always. Our days were happy. Children grew and knew our care. You had forgotten the dark lair of your past, all your prostitute clothing cast in garbage heaps of forgetfulness, or so I thought, or maybe just wished.

You were fished from my bed with the same lure that fed you before, back to the door of paying customers, hustlers and pimps. Temptational, candied filth filled your mouth. You opened your legs to the dregs of violent men. And I found you again, turned back into the repulsive, spitting convulsion like the thing you craved, slaved, and paid your beauty for; once again, a whore.

Oh, Lord, there is no truth or mercy, or intimacy with You in this land. We don't even understand what it means that You're real. We steal and kill for our self-fulfilling wills, eating our fill of each other's adulterous flesh. Fresh and putrid rises the stench as we break free of past restraints, murders piling upon one another. Rage burns for our fellow brother. We smother them with contempt to deaden remorse at how we destroy little boys and girls, corrupt precious, sacred pearls of the future. We have secured a funeral of mourning.

Oh, return to me, Ruhamah. Leave your perversion, your sickly diversion. Remember the embers of my embrace, your tender face, in the place of forgiveness. Until you confess your wrong, turn to the song I am singing, I will expose your lovers, sleeping between your withered breasts. I will uncover your wretched nakedness and shame.

How I long to call you by your name, Ruhamah. My fingers yearn to wash you in the rain, Ruhamah. Here are linen dresses to clothe you in youth, Ruhamah. I have wounded you, but I will heal. It's not pity that I feel as I bandage your lacerations, rub ointment on your contusions and breathe life in your collapsing lungs. You can live with me again, know my touch, be safe, be restored.

I don't want your abstinence sacrifices. I want all of you, America.

Sean is the consummate strategist. He is always analyzing situations and developing searing questions or circumvention. A tremendous athlete, he plays hockey, soccer, golf, badminton and baseball and seems to excel at them all. Sean is presently in Grade 9 and performs all of his schoolwork in his second language which, being from Canada, is French. Sean's attendance at the Wizard Academy's "Young Writer's Workshop" was his first foray into writing in the English language; enjoy.

Curveball

by Sean Fraser

Children playing on streets are prone to being hit by baseballs. I've... er... um... felt it first hand. I used to get hit with baseballs all the time. A few of my school teachers asked me if my parents hit me because I would come to school with so many multicoloured bruises from those baseballs. I lived in downtown New York, right outside of Yankee Stadium. For me, it was magical. I loved the Yankees, especially Babe Ruth. My parents could never afford tickets to watch them play, but I stood outside the stadium just the same to drink in the atmosphere. Every night Babe hit a homerun, I seemed to get hit by a baseball out of nowhere. I was just lucky that way.

... As I was to find out, I would much rather have been hit by baseballs then hang off a cliff 500 feet above the parched dessert...

I was an extremely long way from any sort or sign of civilisation; surrounded by only diabetic cactuses and venomous rattlesnakes. I knew if I lost grip of the ledge, I would soon be gently lifted off to the heavens where I would discover the mystery of death. Although I had great upper body strength, dehydration and near starvation had stolen whatever strength I had left.

I hadn't eaten or drank anything in almost three days. Those days were long, too. So long and excruciating that I probably would've blown my brains out, if I had something to do it with. And there I was, helplessly hanging from a cliff, all because of that mind-boggling mirage.

It danced around, playing with my mind, cackling an evil laugh. My malicious mirage was a tall glass of lemonade. Oh, what I would've done for a glass of bittersweet lemonade straight from Grandpa Jerry's lemon tree. No matter what anyone says, nothing can even come close to the heavenly taste of Grandpa's sweet, sugary lemonade.

The mirage looked so real. I should have known better than to follow a dancing glass of lemonade but my mind was so fried from dehydration that I didn't know what I was doing. It deceived me right over the edge of a cliff!

It's cool how your adrenaline gives you the power to do things you never thought you could do. The rush of adrenaline makes your reaction time so much faster. As soon as I started to fall, I sprang into action, grabbed the ledge and saved my own life. My mind would've never stumbled upon the idea that I could do something like that. It occurred to me that something so incredible only took place in movies; something a superhero would do.

Still hanging, I prayed to god that I'd be safe and a short time later, some incredible force harnessed my strength and I hauled myself up over the ledge to safety. I was so relieved. Although I knew I was going to die sooner or later, I still preferred the reassuring breathes of fresh air; I knew I was still alive.

It was now night time. I nestled down, attempting to remain as warm as I could in the sub-zero temperature. I gazed at the trillions of stars and their formations, pondering all the possibilities as to why god made them in such patterns and figures. I wondered if anyone was watching me this very instant.

Smouldering rage struck me as I recalled the vicious gang that had kidnapped me and left me to parish in this godforsaken desert. They didn't even give me a reason. Regardless, I knew that it was Vinnie Dawnswell's work. I had gotten in some trouble with him at Maxwell Inc., the place where I worked. He showed up and demanded that I give him the blueprints to the project we had been working on for three years and had just finished. I refused and he threatened that there would be trouble if I didn't co-operate. That was a chance I was willing to take so I held my ground.

Later that night, Vinnie's gang broke into my home and kidnapped me. After a couple of hours, driving in the van they had stuffed me in, they shoved me out of the automobile, bound and gagged. Lucky for me, there was a sharp rock lying about fifteen feet away from me. I struggled over to it and sawed off the ropes that bound my hands. Then I untied my legs and the gag around my mouth. Freezing in the pitch black, hypothermic, African desert, I had neither a single crumb of food nor a moist, hydrating drop of fluid of any sort in three torturing days.

I decided that there was no hope for me. I was a goner. Then, rather ironically I began to feel all warm and toasty. My dehydration and hunger were gone. I gazed up in disbelief at a bright, glowing light a short distance away. I did not know what it was until the centre of the light revealed an angel, holding out her hand, asking me to take it and follow her into a magical world. I grasped it gently trailing behind her up to heavens gates.

I would trade death for getting hit by baseballs any day. Heck, I'd trade it for getting bludgeoned by medicine balls.

On the 7th day, God rested. But what about the 8th day? It was the war-crazed Roman emperor Tiberius III who ripped the 8th day off the ancient Sumerian calendar, and the world has wobbled between hope and despair ever since. Those accumulated 8th days, drenched in secrecy and as alive as fingertips, have been safely guarded in a Nepalese grotto ever since.

David Freeman, who co-taught “Wild Fiction,” barely avoided dismemberment when he stole two 8th days at morning twilight. He expended their music on the class of students who wrote this book. The results are evident. Those who write on the 8th day are ignited, and their words toss us like a ball from this world into the next.

THREE STORIES ABOUT THE SUN

by David Freeman

HUMAN RESOURCES MALUNCTION

She was a 114 lb., 28-year-old walking catastrophe. Lindsey had jacked up the calamity factor from "Butterfingers" to "WD40 Paws". How this drove two past boyfriends into the setting sun and marooned her in perpetual singledom is a story for another day.

Retrospectively, Olympic-class clumsiness might not have made Lindsey the best fit for a job as a stewardess.

But she clung to barren optimism like a barnacle to an ugly ship.

British Airways 480 sayonara'ed Heathrow, grabbed air, and full-throttled toward San Francisco. It was Lindsey's first day at work.

The first-class passengers awaited, used to being serviced, lions waiting for meat.

What happened next is best explained with the promotional style of a 50s exploitation flick:

SEE the glass of merlot slide off Lindsey's tray.

GASP as the red wine fans into the air.

HEAR it softly rain down on Alan Kenning's $3800 Brioni suit.

SHRIEK as his head cranes upward and his death stare arrests Lindsey's terror-plagued eyes.

BE AMAZED as time stops for a moment —

— and the torch of love between them is lit.

Some flights have bumpy starts. But if they get you where you really need to go, then the surely you own the sun.

CELEBRATION

I am the sun.
Aching for company, I watched over the land and waters.
My vital light pulled small grasses up until mighty forests grew.
I pulled plankton into fish, and fish into creatures of the sea and air.
I pulled apes out of the trees, and man lit fires in my image.
And I did not stop.
My energy pulled machines into existence, and skyscrapers that tickled the sky.
Man was appreciative, and, though I did not ask or it, he felt compelled to worship me.
He created bombs that borrowed my secrets, which were as bright as my light.
And finally the day of celebration came, when he lit up the skies with a thousand small suns.
And man was no more.

I am the sun.
Aching for company, I watch over the land and waters.

CUTTING

Erin looked in the mirror as the sink filled with warm water. Sometimes she thought she looked okay, although with the tears, she looked goddamn hideous. Probably the ugliest 15-year-old on the planet.

Her therapist didn't understand. Her parents sure didn't.

They always asked the same question: "Why do cut yourself?" How could she tell them the two million reasons, the two million wailing children, the two million nights without sunlight?

It was weird not to hear her parents screaming at each other. They only shut up once a week, when her 13-year-old sister had her singing lesson, like today. Erin was a weed in the asphalt of her family, but Amy found a crack and grew into a broad, white-yellow sunflower. Her heart surprised them all when it tangled itself in, of all things, opera.

The piano music lilted in through the walls. Floating above it, like the dream of an angel, was Amy's voice. Erin knew the music — Puccini's "Un Bel Di" from "Madame Butterfly." Amy had told her that. It was Erin's favorite piece that Amy sung. It coated her bones with kisses and made Erin wish she could fly.

Amy. Who fretted over the perfect cat food for Sparkle. Who put photos of her three favorite suspension bridges on her MySpce page. Who cried when she realized she wasn't strong enough to ever be a professional ballet dancer.

How could this girl Erin had known since her birth make music with a voice so pure that, as Erin listened, a single green tree rose up a thousand miles, with Erin perched on top, caressed by fingers of sun?

If only everything in her world was like that, instead of the heavy black spears that lanced her daily.

The music was perfect, just the thing. Tears still falling, Erin opened up the cabinet doors under the sink and fished out the half-used Kleenex box. She dug down to the bottom and lifted out the razor blade she'd hidden. It was the special one, the one she'd never used. It was the one she kept "just in case."

The wild red that spilled out of her left wrist as she dragged the blade across it was electrically pretty. It was as alive as a sunflower. And then the other wrist. The blood flowed off her white skin, down her fingers. She looked at it with a detached curiosity.

She submerged her wrists and the blood flowed into the warm

water, which had been absorbing her falling tears. The wooziness came easily, like a cat silently entering the room. Amy's voice sounded so sweet...kissing her bones...

The last thing she sensed was the fall, as if suddenly all of her bones had been stolen.

Erin didn't know where she was. The light was clean, like a smile, like the day you know winter is finally gone. The feeling of weightlessness, that was odd, and the lack of anything to see except a blue whiteness. And of course the girl in front of her.

She was pretty. Erin liked the small silver stud on the outside of her right nostril.

"Hi Erin," the girl said. She was younger than Erin. A few inches shorter. She seemed a little sad. "Am I dead?" Erin asked her.

"Yeah," the girl said. "I'm Jessica. I'm supposed to take you to heaven."

"You're an angel?"

The girl nodded. "I died the way you did — I cut myself. Now I guide people to heaven. Mostly cutters."

Erin tried to absorb this. "God will still let us into heaven? I mean, isn't suicide a sin?"

"When I first got here," Jessica said, "I was really confused. I wondered the same thing. This old guy explained why it's okay." Jessica scrunched up her nose, trying to figure out how to put it. "For a long time, people thought God forgot about them. That he didn't care about their problems, or understand. But he did, and when people suffered, he felt it in his heart, the way you would if someone you knew was hurting.

"So he had this idea — he'd put his son — well, it was sort of like a piece of himself — on earth. And make him just like a man, so people could relate. God let them put nails in him and stab him and cut him. God hoped people would see that he understood their suffering, for he suffered more than anyone.

"So…although he got other people to sort of lend a hand, God was the first cutter."

"Did it work?" asked Erin.

Jessica shrugged her shoulders. "Maybe for some. But the world's still screwed up. Cutting doesn't really do much good, it turns out."

"The world is screwed up. And I don't even believe in God." Erin's regret swelled as soon as she'd blurted it out.

Jessica lit a small smile. "I doubt that. God is love. If you've ever experienced love, you've experienced God. Ready to go?"

Erin thought about it. "I guess." She was still trying to adjust. "I'm not going to miss anything down there, that's for sure. Except maybe my sister Amy."

Tears suddenly poured from Erin. Where did these sobs come from that bent her over, that would not cease? Her heart seized in a vice of pain. The salt on her lips, her face wet like a river, and the sobs still ripping through her.

Jessica slipped her warm arms around Erin.

"I miss Amy so much" Erin wailed.

Erin heard a distant voice. It was her sister singing. It roused her from a dark, deep, distant nowhere. Her eyes slowly opened. She's not sure how she got there, on the cold bathroom floor. She was a little lightheaded as she slowly pulled herself to her feet.

She saw the razorblade by the sink filled with clear water. She threw the blade away, drained the water.

Erin pushed herself into the living room. Neither Amy nor her music teacher noticed, both lost in a world of vast golden spaces made of song. Erin's heart rose as she watched Amy's angelic face and listened. Amy's voice ignited the aria, honeying the air with sweet fire.

Amy sensed her, and, still singing, turned and smiled at her sister, whom she loved without limit.

For a moment, Erin thought Amy's face looked like Jessica's. And then it looked like Amy again.

And then, as the music swam in circles around them both, Erin felt lifted, and Amy's face got brighter and brighter, until it was dazzling and dizzy, until there was only an ocean of radiant nothing and everything and forever and so very much sun.

Ray Seggern is best known for discovering 100 different uses for the cashew. Born in 1962 in Baltimore, Maryland, he grew up a military brat and lived on US Navy bases around the globe. He is an avid model railroading enthusiast and volunteer firefighter. He lives in Rapid City, South Dakota with his wife and 6 children, all daughters.

Commonesque

by Ray Seggern

"So," Sadie stated squarely as she stared into the mirror, "whatcha think?'

"I think," her hairdresser replied, "it's your hair. So I want to know: What do *you* think?"

"I think that, umm, well," Sadie paused upon the realization that she did not know what to think of her new electric pink hair. "Hhhhmmmmmm?!"

The pregnant pause allowed the overloud whir of hair dryers and the incessant ringing of phones to invade and interrupt Sadie's thought. In came flooding the other salon sounds: catty conversations and swirling shampoo sinks overlapped and intertwined, ultimately drowned out only by the more palpable silence of her immediate conversational halt.

Sadie stared at the gigantic skull ring that thrust up from the middle finger of her right hand, and which was held in place only with a triple wrap of duct tape on its underside. She spun the ring one complete rotation so that its sunken eyes and Medusa-snake hair again beckoned outward.

After the moment drew overlong, the stylist offered a prompt. "Pink is what you asked for, remember?"

Sadie replied, grasping for a sophistication exceeding the grasp of her eleven years, "Oh whatta they call it? 'buyer's…regret?'"

"Remorse" the stylist countered, running his hand through his slightly spiky/receding plume. "The term is 'buyer's remorse,'"

"Remorse?" she contemplated the word. "Hmmmmmmm?!"

The stylist offered whatever he could muster in the way of reassurance. "Well, they always say it is better to regret something you *have* done, instead of something you haven't."

The pre-teen girl slumped further into the barber's chair, taking mental inventory of her new 'do as her slouch curved ever more.

"Besides, your mom will love it," he said, her smile widening in the oval mirror.

Sadie shot back, "which I guess explains your willingness to, umm, help."

The stylist flashed his own smile, signifying his role in the conspiracy. The sound of a repeatedly honking car horn cuts through the continued cacophony of the salon.

"Sounds like your mom," the stylist said.

"What, remorse?"

"No, your mom" he replied, laughing. "she's in the parking lot, honking her horn."

"Riiiiiiiight," she said, hopping up from the chair and grabbing her backpack from the corner, knowing this is her cue for one last piece of business before her exit. "So…Dad…about my shoes?"

Half expecting this was coming, he reached inside his stylist's smock and cups both hand over his fanny pack, as though he were girding his loins for the shakedown, this monetary, psychological warfare that the father and daughter engaged in every other weekend and two weeks each summer.

"How much?" he asked.

"Don't you even wanna see em?" Sadie replied with faux-indignation, shuffling through her backpack to produce a low-res ink jet printout of the shoes.

"Let me guess, they're 'rad,' right?" he said condescendingly, before returning to the financial issue in near-military cadence.

"How. Much."

"Forty! Nine!" Sadie replied, imitating his tone and tenor.

"Fifty? Awww jeez Sadie, can't you ask your Mom pay for that?"

"Dad, You *know* how she is."

"Yeah…ya think?"

The dad and daughter headed for the parking lot and he slipped her a neatly folded fifty dollar bill, which she discretely pocketed as they head out the door. A fresh cigarette dangled from his lips as they head into the parking lot.

"So, you're headed to your Mee Maw's today, I suspect, being Saturday?"

"I wish that me and you could spend more time together," she said.

"Yeah, well, talk to your mom's lawyer about that," he replied, his ex-wife now coming into focus across the parking lot.

"I think they're dating." She offered. "Maury."

The hairstylist paused at the realization. "Well that explains a lot,"
The two former lovers come face to face in the middle of the parking lot. They square up to each other and stare, standing ten paces apart, neither one wanting to blink first. As Sadie emerges from her father's shadow, the impact of Sadie's new hairdo becomes obvious on her mom's face.

"Oh no…No, no, no, no, NO!" The ex-wife screamed, her index finger windshield-wipering in perfect synchronicity with her Negative Nancy nod.

"You know you're just encouraging her."

"Funny, I think encouragement is a good thing," he said, pulling a deep puff of his cigarette and taunting a plume of secondhand smoke toward her. The mother feigned a fake cough toward her ex-husband and then glared her trademark scowl of disapproval toward Sadie, who in turn plodded and plopped herself toward the backseat of her mother's Chevy Tahoe.

The mother's glare grew fiery, now diverted through the rearview mirror.

"So what do you call that look you're cultivating there?"

"I dunno…" Sadie, replied, rolling her eyes.

The mother pulled the Tahoe into Drive. Then, while driving *and* shuffling for a year-old pack of cigarettes in the glove compartment, she caught a glimpse of her daughter in the rearview. "I saw that. Don't you *daaaare* roll your eyes at me."

"Nah, I'd never do that. It's just that a bug flew in. I think it was a locust," Sadie replied in full smartass mode. "Yeah a locust. How

many locusts does it take to make a swarm? How 'bout a plague? That's more than a swarm, right?"

The mother found the ripe pack of smokes and now flicked and flecked at the even older lighter, unsuccessfully. As he continued in her attempt to light up a cigarette, unsuccessfully, Sadie saw the opportunity to pile on.

"Ah, you've started smoking again. Very nice. I'm hearing reeeeeeally good things about it from that camel on the billboard."

"I haven't… started… smoking… cuz… this… damn… lighter… won't…"

There was an awkward pause and then, making contact through the rearview, the two erupted into laughter simultaneously. The mother abandoned her attempt to light the cigarette, the craving having passed, her thumb raw in defeat.

Sadie acknowledged this change in the conversational weather as her chance to broach a new subject.

"So, Mom, I need to get some new shoes,"

"Aww Sadie, can't you ask your dad for that stuff, just once?

"Mom, *you know how he is.*"

"Hmmmmmph...*You think*?" her mother replies.

The Tahoe pulled into an apartment complex and rolled to a stop in the handicapped parking spot.

"So Mom," she pleaded, "you should come in for awhile. We'll have a good old-fashioned girl party. What was that movie you and Mee Maw used to watch when you were a little girl?"

"Aw honey, that's sweet, but you know I can't. Now be sure to get Mee Maw to drive you to the store. And get something presentable," the mother rattled off, "Puh-leeeeez none of those horrible skating shoes this time."

The Mother grabbed her purse to produce a crisp 50-dollar bill.

"I'm not wild about that hair—*or that ring*—but we can talk about it tomorrow."

"Yes Mommy," Sadie mumbled as she piled out the car-door with her backpack in tow. "Love you Mommy."

That familiar smell of macaroni tickled Sadie's nose as she entered the apartment. The other benchmark of her Mee Maw's place was the always-playing radio in the corner, always tuned to her sermons.

"We are failing our children," the radio voice preached, "and in turn they are failing us."

The other thing that was striking and unforgettable was her "roommates," dozens of figurines of animals, all in matching sets: zebras and elephants giraffes and cows and pigs. Every species known to man, ever, seemed to roost or nest or otherwise habitate somewhere here in the old lady's lair. It was if Noah's passenger manifest were shrunken and fired and glazed to a dull semi-gloss finish. Sadie could think back, just barely, to the days when she used to play 'make believe' with the assorted animals, when they had names and made up back-stories and she would breathe life into them. Now, that seemed like a long time ago. And here, and now, they seemed lifeless by comparison.

Scattered among the figurines were pictures of Mee

Maw and her long-dead husband--Sadie's Paw Paw--who was killed in the Vietnam war long before Sadie was even born. Strikingly absent were pictures of Sadie's own mother, save for a single infant photo.

Sadie honed in on tattered 5 x 8 black-and-white photo of a young Paw Paw, young and handsome and vital in his dress blues. After a moment of admiration, she eventually saluted the picture.

Mee Maw lay fast asleep on her couch with a collector's guide tented across her stomach. Seeing that, Sadie focused in on a set of small porcelain horses, lined tightly together in formation on the mantle. Sadie nudged the figurines left and right, as to make a space for another figurine to be placed right in the middle.

She then slid quietly to sit on the coffee table and looks at her Mee Maw. She reached out her right hand to trace the outline of Mee Maw's face, the oversized ring averting her gaze. As Sadie's hand gently bumped MeeMaw's cheek, the grandmother awoke.

"Well hello my angel."

"Surprise, surprise."

"Well indeed it is."

"So Mom's going with her new boyfriend," Sadie said, "Anyway…She said I need some new shoes. Said that I could just ride my bike.

"Ohhhh. OK. Need some money?"

"Yes please, Mee Maw."

"Well, hand me my purse sweetheart"

Sadie shuffled her grandmother the purse. The old lady fumbled and struggled to put her glasses on. "Mee-Maw's eyesight ain't as good as it once was," the old lady commented in self-deprecation.

Sadie smiled as her grandmother produced a crisp fifty dollar bill. "Thanks Mee-Maw. You're the best. 'Bout an hour, OK."

"Ohhhhhh-kay."

Sadie peddled her beat-up bike through the neighborhood, eventually arriving at Sonny's Vintage store. Sadie ambled the bike up to the door, ditched it, and burst in through the front door furiously.

The sales counter is manned by Sonny himself, a pauncy, fifty-ish Jewish man. He recognized the girl immediately. "Well well well, Sadie Hawkins."

"Wow, that's really clever and original," Sadie volleyed back with her trademark sarcasm.

As Sadie approached the counter, seeing the height imbalance, she slid a chair over to bring her equal in height to the junk peddler. Sadie scanned the glass display case for a particular piece, a small porcelain pony, which she recognized immediately.

"It looks just like it did last week," the old man retorted. "It hasn't sprouted wings…or horns."

"Today's the day Sonny."

"Really?"

Sonny produced the figurine. Sadie inspected it carefully, squinting to make sure it was the genuine artifact, which she knew was signified by a particular lilt to the "J" in the artists' signature, Jobert.

"Most people would say, "JOB-uhrt," Sadie suggested, "but it is really pronounced "zho-BAIR."

"If you don't mind me asking, really, how does such a young lady develop such an inquisite interest in post-war oriental collectibles, and really expensive ones at that."

"Nah, that's my Paw Paw. He started buying 'em for my Mee Maw in the war. Vietnam."

"Oh I've heard of it."

Sadie thumbed through her money, stashing back one of the three fifties she had acquired today, sliding the other two across the counter toward Sonny.

"Fifties, eh? You didn't rob a liquor store did you?"

"It's from my parents."

"Well that's generous, buying your grandma such a nice gift."

"It's the least they could do," she said with a sly grin.
"The very least.

"Actually I'm pretty sure they all hate each other."

"I see," the vendor replied, not knowing the full gravity of the remark or how to respond.

"So Sonny, I need you to do me a solid here. Y'know, now that I'm a high roller…a big spender and all," the girl implored. "Can you throw in one of those ratty pair of hand-me-down tennies back there?"

"Well, okay," he contemplated. "I'm not usually in the business of giving things away. But I suppose it's the…"

After a pause, the two finish his sentence in stereo, chuckling, "least I could do."

"So Sadie Hawkins, what kinda shoes do you want?"

"I dunno. Whatcha got?"

Sadie followed Sonny's directions and walked to the shoe aisle tucked among the other clothing items in the back of the store. In a row of secondhand athletic shoes, she identified a gently worn pair of black and white checkered Vans shoes. The price tag on the bottom of the shoes says "$5"

"Perfect," Sadie mumbles.

Heading out the store, she perched herself beneath the neon beer lights in the window just long enough to switch the pricetag from the shoes and tape it to the figurine. With the slightest slight of hand, the "expensive oriental collectible" was suddenly a piece of pawn shop junk.

The sun was setting as Sadie finally made it back to Mee Maw's apartment. She reentered to again find the fragile old lady asleep on the couch. Sadie again walk immediately to the picture of her Paw Paw, and again saluted. "Mission accomplished!"

She joined her grandmother on the couch, waking her. "You're not going to believe what I found," she exclaimed, producing the figurine, which generated an simultaneous glean of recognition and confusion from the grandmother, as it matched one of the prized, but incomplete series displayed prominently on the mantle.

"Well I'll be," the old woman flustered. "Do you know how long I've been looking for that?"

"You know I do," Sadie replied.

"But that had to cost…"

"Nope," Sadie interjected, cutting Mee Maw off in mid-sentence. "Thrift store. Check it."

Sadie turned over the figurine to show the avid collector the price tag she had just switched from the cheapie shoes she bought. "Here, put on your glasses."

Mee Maw turned over the small horse to reveal that it was, in fact, a numbered Jobert original, signed by the artist, and that the girl had seemingly found it for only five dollars.

"Well it's a miracle," Mee Maw stammered. "That's what it is. A miracle."

"Go put her with the rest of 'em," Sadie suggested

Mee Maw walked toward the shelf where the collection rested above her empty apartment fireplace. While Mee Maw wasn't looking, Sadie slipped Mee Maw's original fifty dollar bill back into her purse, unannounced and unnoticed.

Mee Maw paused noticing the new space in the section where the incomplete Jobert Equine Collection had heretofore been so tightly nestled. With a knowing glance over the shoulder, she played into Sadie's scenario. "Looks like they're expecting her."

Mee Maw beamed admiring her now complete collection.

"When Paw-paw and I were courting…he was stationed overseas of course," Mee-maw paused, tears welling in her eyes. "And every time he'd come home he'd bring me…"

After a few seconds, Sadie attempted to save her grandma from the moment and change the subject.

"How about my shoes. Cool, right?" Sadie propped both shoes up on the coffee table, tapping her toes together repeatedly.

Mee Maw was now back in the moment, wiping the tears from her cheek, now completely focused on her granddaughter. "You bet they are."

"Well thanks for buying 'em for me, Mee Maw. I don't know what I'd do without you. Mom and Dad act like they don't even care."

"Well, I just want you to get what you need. And don't be mad at them. It's a tough time. Anyways, *you know how they are.*"

"You think?" Sadie replied smiling.

"I think that tonight," Mee Maw exclaimed, "we should make a biiiiig batch of tollhouse cookies.

"Oooh. Yeah yeah yeah, with the big chocolate chunks," Sadie concurred. "And you know what we haven't watched in awhile?"

"What's that?"

"Breakfast at Tiffany's."

"Well you know that's your Mee Maw's favorite," the old woman replied. "Sounds like a girl party to me."

Mee Maw smiled, patting Sadie on the thigh. As they held hands, Sadie's skull ring dwarfs her grandma's weather wedding band. Sadie lay her head on her the old woman's shoulder.

"Mee-maw, you're my best friend."

"Well, then that makes me the luckiest grandma in the old folk's home."

"You don't live in an *old folks home*."

Mee Maw chuckled, stroking Sadie's face and hair, her gentle old hand tracing the outline of her face.

"Oh my sweet sweet Sadie," Mee Maw said, basking in the moment of sheer companionship.

"Now, you know, Mee Maw's eyesight ain't as good as it once was, but tell me…

"…is your hair…?"

"Yeah, pink," Sadie replied.

Alexandria Young is a pale teen from a small dusty town nowhere near where you live. She spends the vast majority of her time slaying dragons, killing bosses, and disco dancing in a nearby village. She's a shy girl who much prefers the company of books over humans, though from time to time she can be found in the presence of certain gnomish persons, enjoying tea and exchanging warlike banter.

"Ruby Stained"

-Alexandria Young

The woman-child sat in a field of green. Her long, black hair reached down her back. Two black wings rested between her shoulder-blades, and black feathers covered them. A long tail arched behind her head, demonic.

"So you've come to end this at last." she said to someone behind me, "I know you're there, Father, come out so I can see your face before you murder me."

A man walked out of the woods to the south-east. "You call me Father and all I've ever done is hunted you." the man said.

"I know my existence is wrong." She said in an angry voice. "Tell me, when you have finished killing me, who will be sent to kill you? Surely They won't let the monster that created the mongrel live?"

I turned to see what reaction the man would have to her words. He was as different from his daughter as day is from night. Short, light blond hair and white feathers in his arching wings, no tail. "I have no wish to kill you, but-"

The young woman interrupted him: "You have no choice if you want to live? Have you ever thought maybe the life of your child is worth more than your own?"

The woman looked almost in pain. I turned away, unable to watch. As the man approached her, the woman began to look younger, almost a child. He drew a sword from a baldric between his wings, his face fighting with what was right and what would save his own life.

I turned away before he struck her. The last image I saw was the woman-child sitting in the field of green, her ebon wings stained ruby.

I kept it a secret. I was five years old. Shooting the PB pier, I face planted into a barnacle-encrusted pylon. I almost drowned. Rachel saved my life. She was a Risso's dolphin, divorced with two calves, Ryan and Lois. Turns out I was gifted. I spoke perfect dolphinese. Later, I wrote a screenplay loosely based on my dolphin speaking skills. Perhaps you've heard of it, **Ace Ventura Pet Detective**.

High School was either boring or I was slooowww. Or maybe my self-euthanized brain cells outnumbered my good citizen cells. Anyway, whatever dude, I graduated in 1974. Seven years later, I wrote my second screenplay, loosely based on what I think I remembered. I called it, **Fast Times At Ridgemont High**? I really went to Clairemont High, just changed the first part of the name. Get it? Yeah, I know. Confusing. Huh? What was I talkin about? Let's move on. I enlisted. The Army shipped me to the Cold War Epicenter, West Berlin. All believed I was a simple-minded, fast fingered, 127 words per minute, typist/personnel clerk. Ha, ha, that was the perfect cover for a deadly handsome Top-Secret-Double-Agent-Agent. Every wonder why the Berlin Wall **really** fell? Hello? At the tender age of twenty, I was awarded the Good Conduct Medal, The Medal Of Honor and an Honorable Discharge. Twenty-three years later, I penned yet another screenplay, loosely based on my experiences. You guessed it, **The Bourne Identity.**

I returned to San Diego and re-enlisted in the US Navy. I was stationed in Miramar. Ever heard of the Navy Fighter Weapons School. Umm-hmm, that was me too! Six years later, I had the need for speed, got that loving feeling and wrote the whole thing in under seventeen hours. I went simple, just called it - **Top Gun.**

Cocaine raged in the 80's. I went Marian Trench undercover with the DEA. I JENGAed their downfall. Noriega, Kaiser Souza and Pablo Escobar – TIMBER! My work was stain dark and oily. In Rehab, I twitched and toiled for nine months, exorcising demons the only way I know. I authored a set of screenplays, loosely based on my experiences. Maybe you know someone who's seen the movie versions? **Pulp Fiction, The Usual Suspects and Scar Face.**

I am a close personal friend with Dr. Dink Weber

What next? Ask my neighbors and they'll describe me like others describe postal workers, balding maintenance men and dumb ass power-ball lottery winners. They'd comment, "**He was quiet and monkish. Kept to himself. A friendly fellow.**" Yeah, that's me all right. Mr. Average. Quietly bleeding out on my next screenplay, a prequel -- **Love Splinters and Invisible Bruising.**
Check it...**boo-yah-ka-shaw**! Snap!

Love Splinters and Invisible Bruising

by Ken Brand

Dad wore four tattoos. Two were unremarkable.

The third covered his right shoulder. Inked exquisitely in burning shades of China red, deep shadowy greens and sinful blacks, he grinned. Hidden like deceit, in the fine detail of leered expression, tall feline limbs stretched Y'd. Eager delicate fingers wrapped hard round his harder horns. She draped. Ripe. Lithe. Bareback. Wearing only a soft seductive smile, Eve rode the serpent's forked tongue. Like he knew your sins, Lucifer grinned.

The fourth? Colors of bruising. Deep purples, blackened blues and tints of jaundiced yellows. Although this tattoo was invisible, it was as real and heavy as shackle iron. A thick blue hourly-wage-slave collar encircled dad's throat.

Dad never finished high school, ran hot, got caught, did time, met mom, and married her, my sister, and me. The DNA of addiction colored our bloods and dad's obsessions shined and shadowed our family in equal measure. Family in-tow, he cinched his noosed collar tight and strapped himself down tighter. Beyond reason, he worked hardest, partied harder and played hard. My dad was a complicated man and dangerous.

SHINED SUN
Outdoors it rained sheets of shined sun.

From our terraced backyard, Tecolote Canyon sprawled napping while tall San Diego skies melted into a shiny sea-blue tabletop. The Coronado Islands were plainly visible.

From our front yard, a confetti of pastel house hues, neated lawns, garden gnomes, chrome grilled automobiles, wild flowers and people pollen, breezed across the sweeping hillside, then splashed laughing into the blue glitter of Mission Bay.

It rained sheets of shine and confetti outdoors. Indoors, currents of pressured tension, contangoed danger and awkward love, whipsawed, bone rattled, convulsed and wept without warning.

We didn't "walk on eggshells"; we played hide-n-go-seek, tiptoeing through a house crammed with randomly armed, hidden and half hidden emotional land mines. There was bloodshed and heartache, scarring and love splinters.

BARE FEET

Our shouts and flapping arms only speedballed his rabbit panic. "STOP!!!! DONT RUNNNN", we screamed in karaoke. Running from dad or trouble was always a mistake. Erich squirted through the half closed sliding glass door, sprinting crouched, zigity-zag beneath the heavily fruited trees. Uniformly trimmed limbs kept in-chase dad at arms length and Erich momentarily shadowed in safety. Half hurrying, Dad rounded the peach tree, nearly tripping on the shit shovel. He skidded, stepped backwards and scooped up the shovel.

Moments and my breath compressed. My body paralyzed, my worries shot ahead. I was a goner. I knew it. Our dogs crapped everywhere. Policing the backyard, shoveling-up the squishy turd piles and heaving them into the canyon was one of my daily chores. The shit shovel laying in the yard, not neatly stored in its tool shed place, was easily worth a few lashes from dad's skinny brown belt. If his bare feet stepped in a fresh shit pile, dog shit I was supposed to have previously policed, I'd be covered in belt welts for certain.

With a looping one-handed arc, the smooth side of the shovel found it's tiny bulls eye. Erich's four-year-old kid self levitated, cannonballing into harsh sunlight. Shocked, mom and dad raced to collect and inspect him. Injuries included only utter confusion, heaved sobbing and slobber. His original infraction pardoned, further punishment was deemed unnecessary. Erich had learned a hard lesson, a lesson the rest of us Brand kids already knew; "Flinching was allowed. Never break and run; always stand your ground."

Collecting myself, I hustled into the canyon, huffing into the wind, "Dear Jesus, thank you for not letting dad step in dog shit. I promise to pray more and beat the crap out of my sister less. Amen." and wondering, "Why was dad was barefoot?"

RULES OF ENGAGEMENT

I've seen furniture splintered, tables cracked in two and objects flying. I've watched dad's skinny brown belt whistle and crack, and I've worn welts myself. I've witnessed hateful word-to-word combat and an occasional grapple.

Once, mid meltdown, mom stormed down the hallway. Dad followed. She slammed the door in his face and locked him out. Without a word or warning, he hip-snapped a haymaker, blowing his balled fist and splintered wood chunks through an eight-inch hole. Calmly, he reached through, unbolted the door and let himself in. I was more impressed than petrified. That same hallway has three bullet holes.

I've seen plenty, but I've never seen dad hit my mom. A rule of engagement, I supposed, one on a short-list of Brand Family Geneva Conventions.

FIRE STICKS

It began like you might strike a campfire, by furiously rubbing two dry sticks together. Friction first, then heat, expectant sparks, measured fanning, stoke with flammables and Eureka! Licking flames. Only mom and dad weren't lighting a cozy campfire, nobody sang Kum-By-Ya or served S'mores. This fire leapt fierce and hostile.

Mom spoke harshly, rubbing dad wrong. Dad chaffed back and mom bit deeper. Dad blared hotter. Mom reflected his heat and lobbed a few flammables for good measure. Dad detonated, spun to the counter, snatched up the dinner dishes, cranked them over his head and wheeled to face mom. Flinching, her silver sandaled feet fell back two steps. Blocked by the wall, she fumbled behind herself, frantic hands seeking the rake.

With a two-fisted chokehold, she whipped the wood handled rake between her and dad. Screwed into the business end was an immense fanning, white plastic rake head. Dad smashed the dishes to the floor. Mom shielded herself with the rake. I tensed transfixed. Cheap dishes exploded like frozen ice. Sharp edged, ill shaped shrapnel skittered across the linoleum. Peeking behind shag rake tines, mom yipped, "God Damn You". Dad didn't say a word. He just growled, stepping a pace closer to mom and directly in front of the harvest gold stove.

On the right back burner sat mom's pride, dad's recent anniversary present. Like a J.C. Penney museum piece, gleaming in Scandia White, glazed with graceful stems of soft blue, tender blue leaves and blooming blue daisies, sat mom's Corning Ware coffee carafe. Wrapping his fist around the thin stainless steel handle, he jerked the piece over his head and glared directly into mom's brown eyes.

She stiffened, dropped her tined shield below her chin, dropped her tone two octaves and threatened dad, "Don't you DAARRREEE!" Dad rocked back three inches. His cocked arm froze; Lucifer peeked from beneath dad's white short sleeve. Dad's head swiveled right, our wide eyes glancing off each other. His ricocheted left, mine right and we both locked on mom, glaring and daring.

Patterns broke, awareness doused his flames and dad gently reset the carafe. Wheeling, he brushed by me, lightly squeezing my left shoulder. As he walked out, smoke wisps and flecks of soot curled softly in his wake. The screen door slammed. Mom wept and broomed, I collected the bigger shards with her rake.

Silently, I wondered why they couldn't just stop rubbing their fire sticks together? I was grateful that as hot as it got, there were rules of engagement.

LOS LOCOS

Dad was de facto capo of the Los Locos Motorcycle Club, a crash of
cronies race'n wide open. Founding members included dad, eight initiated work buddies and my two favorite uncles. Uncle Ryan cracked the funniest jokes, was a part time barber, genius motorcycle mechanic and an ex con. He told me he was innocent, of what, nobody would say. The men had nicknames. Uncle Ryan's was "Blue". Uncle Sonny's was "Torp"; he was an honest-to-God, fully commissioned, US Navy Submarine Commander.

On any Sunday, Los Locos and occasional uninitiated friends chewed up the Miramar Canyons, racing tweaked out two strokes and bored out thumpers. After burning through beer, breaking down or crashing too hard, the tribe frequently rallied to secret and randomly rotating locations. Habitually, severe partying ensued, gnarly stories were told and history rewritten. On just such an occasion, the after party crash-landed at our house. I leaned in the shadows. Watching without speaking, Dad had a strict kid law, "Do not speak unless spoken to."

I laughed inside my head at the stories dad's drunken friends told or more usually, slurred. Dad was a good listener, never laughed too loud, shined an occasional approving half smile and sporadically snorted, "bullshit". Mostly, dad was quiet; he didn't approve of bragging. Many of the stories others told included dad in the telling.

A friend of Blue's, a guy called "Duce", was a loud mouth. I'd never seen him before and he obviously didn't know dad. I couldn't make out Duce's words, but his tone was clear and I could read his animated body language; he spoke disrespectfully -- twice. I unleaned, attentive. Dad's smile flattened and his relaxed posture rippled slightly. I'd seen this before and I suspected what Duce did not.

It took five heartbeats. Grabbing a fist full of shirt collar and a handful of belt, dad spun him, jerked him six inches off his feet and launched him head first through the closed screen door. Torn from its hinges, Duce followed the bent doorframe. Crumpled man and metal cart wheeled down the front porch steps and skidded to a rude stop on the front lawn. The door was a total loss; Duce wore fresh grass stains, a bleeding forehead and newfound respect. I thought, "He knows dad now." He left quietly. On the hi-fi, Mick leaned into "Get off my cloud" and the sounds of drunken story telling swallowed the pause. Before things really got out of hand, I slipped out the back door.

HIGH SIERRAS

Among the initiated and the left behind, Los Locos annual crusades were legend. Desert racing in Baja, deep sea fishing expeditions, hell raising at McQueen's Elsinore Gran Prix, and the most epic of all, a sons included, deep into the High Sierras, week-long motorcycle camping trip.

From base camp, eleven crazies and their thirteen sons strapped a weeks worth on our backs and bikes. Swift kick starts cranked hostile horsepower to combat. With nodded smiles, as one, gloved fingers stretched, then squeezed clutch. Booted toes mashed gears to engagement. Twenty-four wrists wrenched throttles full-bore. Agitated sounds of tuned engines, straining metal and hot exhaust swarmed like flying scorpions, stabbed stinging through whispering pines, hived up the mountainside and disappeared into formerly silent canyons.

Charging single file, blurred silver spokes pounded down thin trails, scratched up ravines, rounded blind corners and bounced over stumps. Dodging half boulders and splashing through rushing streams, our horde hauled ass it's six-hour way to Grasshopper Flats, Eden on earth.

We camped on twenty yards of velvety grass surrounded by a weave of ancient and holy pines. Ninety paces into the forest, rich earth turned to boulders and slabs of smoothed rock. The Kern River flexed, awed, ripped and roared. Down stream, in eddied pools and fingered streams, rainbowed trout schooled, eager and unwise.

In daylight, we fished, caught, rode and napped. We boys also gathered wood.

At dusk, we gorged on endless pan-fried trout, sunflower seeds and beef jerky.

At night our bonfire threw strobed shadows, floated sparks and crackled like broken bones. Inky black hid behind star blaze and random meteors bottle rocketed across the sky.

Curled safely in our sleeping bags, we soaked in the familiar. Loud laughing and Wild Turkey fueled story telling. Charred wood smells, campfire smoke, the clean scent of pine trees and the heady aroma of burning weed. There were also hooting owls and occasional gunfire.

One night a debate flared. The question? Who was the greatest heavyweight; Joe Frazier or Cassius Clay? It turned personal, as things often do when men are too stoned to stand, then physical.

Blue: *"Ali was a deserter and big mouth punk!"*

Wing Nut: *"He wasn't a deserter, he was a conscious observer. You're a dumb ass!"*

Angel: *"Smoken'n Joe was a righteous puncher brother, he'd take your head of with one punch!"*

Torp: *"Are you two dumb asses related to Gomer Pyle? It's conscientious objector you moron. Sent his ass to prison, shoulda shot him as a traitor. Boy could box though."*

Wing Nut: *"Fuck you all, I'm not a dumb ass, mother fuckers, believe that!"*

Two Shoes: "*No, fuck you, mutha fucker, shut your pie hole!*"

Ringo: "*You're the punk! You ever even been in a fight -- whatchu know bout fighten -- my wife could kick your ass.*"

Two Shoes: "*I can kick your ass. I know that! And yer drunk anyway.*"

Ringo: "*Yeah, well you can't ride for shit asshole! And I'm not drunk Goober, I'm* high *therz a difference shit for brains and I know what you don't know, you knowww?*"

Squeak, thinking he was the Sheriff, stood, wobbled, righted himself, pulled his short-barreled Smith & Wesson and fired one shot in the air and two through the green tin Coleman stove. Dad and Wing Nut leapt to their feet, others dove to the ground and some gawked, like us. They tackled him, rolled half into the fire and threw punches. It ended as fast as it started.

The next morning, you'd never know anything unusual had happened, because it hadn't. Dad's knuckles were scraped, Wing Nut's pinky finger was dislocated and Squeak wore a singed shirt, a purple eye and a sheepish grin. His morning mantra, "*What the fuck, I was just try'n to restore a little order.*"

Sons were taught how to fish, how to start a fire, other stuff and simple camping laws. Laws like "*Don't point a gun at anyone, even if you think it's unloaded,*" and "*Shared stories and deeds done were considered "Camp Talk"*. "*Camp Talk*" was never shared with the women. Not mothers, not sisters, not girlfriends. Never.

Breaking the "*don't point*" law might earn a beat down, even if you point at the sky or a stove; breaking the "*Camp Talk Law*" was more painful. My friend Johnny, Ringo's son, found out the hard way. One year he broke the "*Camp Talk*" law, the next year he was left behind with his mom and sisters. My brothers and I made every trip.

BOYHOOD ENDS

I worked at dad's printing factory as the weekend janitor and gofer. A full time ~~wageslaveship~~ apprenticeship would begin mere days after my graduation. As doomsday neared, the dread of working in dad's salt mine shoved me to action. Three months before graduation, without permission, I enlisted in the US Army. Because I was seventeen, I needed signatures. Fearing slave hood more than dad's disapproval and danger, I waited two weeks before ceremonies to pronounced my decision and request he sign my permission slip. I braced dad in his woodworking shop and was prepared to demand it. Dad locked eyes with me and said, "*I'm glad you're not going into this blood sucking business Kenny. You're a smart boy, son. Learn a skill, travel the world, meet pretty girls, become a man.*" Relief vertigo almost dropped me. When we told mom, she blubbered tears and hugged me so hard it hurt.

Tuesday evening, August 12th, 1974, I tossed my duffle bag into the trunk, we loaded into the Pontiac Le Mans and drove to the downtown Grey Hound Station. I hugged Terri, Jay and Erich, kissed mom and dad. One last time, I punched Teri and Jay in the shoulder, turned and bounded up the steps, nearly tripping.

Pulling away, Teri and Jay were bickering as usual; little Erich waved. Mom's chin trembled as she dabbed tears. Dad looked taller. His right arm hugged mom tightly. He waved, launched a lazy left-handed semi salute and cracked an approving half smile. The brand of smile I'd only ever seen him share with the men he worked and played with, and now me.

—The End

Live Your Crowded Hour

Standing at your bedside, I don't know if you're dead or only sleeping.

Soon our friends will lay pennies on your eyes to pay Charon for your passage. A silly ritual, our friends will do it anyway.

But you were dead long before you died.

Something caused life to shrivel in you, bloodless and pale, until you began to smell of despair. Did fear of failure run so deep in you?

I was troubled by your passivity. I did not understand it. You refused encouragement. You sneered at good advice. You drank self-pity until it pickled your soul.

Did you never realize that He who gently made the lamb made the tiger also? Who strangled the tiger in you? Was it faulty religion? An overbearing parent? Wounded pride?

The tiger who fails is still a tiger. We do not laugh at it. A tiger is spectacular.

You understood the Jesus who turned water into wine at the wedding feast to save the young couple from embarrassment. You believed in that Jesus, the one who was kind and anonymously generous. But you never quite believed in the Jesus who braided a whip to drive the businessmen from the temple, who flung aside the tables of the moneychangers and scattered their cash and stampeded all their livestock.

Was there human blood on the whip when he was done do you think? Or did he just wave the whip over his head like a baton twirler in a halftime show and request that all the nasty, bad men please leave the premises immediately?

Jesus wasn't Gandhi. Jesus said that when someone jolted your jaw, the right thing to do was look them calmly in the eye and stick out your chin to give them a clean swing at the other side. This is how a tiger says, "Is that your best shot? You want another swing? Here, let me make this easy for you."

Turning the other cheek isn't submissive. It's defiant.

But you were never into defiance. You were more into whining.

I wish I could say I will miss you. But in truth, I've been missing you since the day your tiger died.

— Roy H. Williams

Tiger Mending, by Amy Cutler

What is Wizard Academy?

Composed of a fascinating series of workshops led by some of the most accomplished instructors in America, Wizard Academy is a progressive new kind of business and communications school whose stated objective is to improve the creative thinking and communication skills of sales professionals, internet professionals, business owners, educators, ad writers, ministers, authors, inventors, journalists and CEOs.

Founded in 1999, the Academy has exploded into a worldwide phenomenon with an impressive fraternity of alumni who are rapidly forming an important worldwide network of business relationships.

"Alice in Wonderland on steroids! I wish Roy Williams had been my very first college professor. If he had been, everything I learned after that would have made a lot more sense and been a lot more useful... Astounding stuff."

—Dr. Larry McCleary,
Neurologist and Theoretical Physicist

"...Valuable, helpful, insightful, and thought provoking. We're recommending it to everyone we see."
—Jan Nations and Sterling Tarrant
senior managers, Focus on the Family

"Be prepared to take a wild, three-ring-circus journey into the creative recesses of the brain...[that] will change your approach to managing and marketing your business forever. For anyone who must think critically or write creatively on the job, the Wizard Academy is a must."

—Dr. Kevin Ryan
Pres., The Executive Writer

"Even with all I knew, I was not fully prepared for the experience I had at the Academy... Who else but a wizard can make sense of so many divergent ideas? I highly recommend it."

—Mark Huffman,
Advertising Production Manager, Procter & Gamble

"A life-altering 72 hours."

—Jim Rubart

To learn more about Wizard Academy, visit www.WizardAcademy.org or call the academy at (800) 425-4769